# HISTORIC OKLAHOMA COUNTY

## An Illustrated History
### by Pendleton Woods

*Best regards for Jerry Jensen    Pendleton Woods*

Published for the Oklahoma City/County Historical Society

Historical Publishing Network
A division of Lammert Publications, Inc.
San Antonio, Texas

Oklahoma 2007 Centennial

*An aerial view of the destruction of the Alfred P. Murrah Federal Building after a bomb was detonated outside the building on April 19, 1995.*
COURTESY OF THE CITY OF OKLAHOMA CITY.

ISBN: 1-893619-25-7
Library of Congress Card Catalog Number: 2002103151

### Historic Oklahoma County: An Illustrated History

| | |
|---|---|
| *author:* | Pendleton Woods |
| *editor:* | William D. Welge |
| *cover artist:* | Greg Burns |
| *contributing writers for "Sharing the Heritage":* | Pendleton Woods, Eric Dabney |

### Historical Publishing Network

| | |
|---|---|
| *president:* | Ron Lammert |
| *vice president:* | Barry Black |
| *project managers:* | Lou Ann Murphy |
| *director of operations:* | Charles A. Newton, III |
| *administration:* | Angela Lake |
| | Donna M. Mata |
| | Dee Steidle |
| *graphic production:* | Colin Hart, John Barr, Mike Reaves |

Printed and bound in Spain by Bookprint, S.L., Barcelona

# CONTENTS

*A bird's eye view of Oklahoma City looking from the northwest in the late 1890s.*

# FROM THE AUTHOR

The story of Oklahoma County is unique in many ways. Perhaps its most unique quality is that its county seat—Oklahoma City—is the only major city in the world literally settled by a race into the territory. We would like to say "horse race," but most of the people coming to Oklahoma City during the Run came by the Santa Fe Railroad. The train left the starting point at the same moment horses moved out, but was not allowed to travel any faster than a horse could run.

However, the uniqueness of the county seat, which became the State Capital, extends beyond its original settlement.

In barely more than ten years after the town was carved from raw prairie land, it would boast an opera house with the largest stage west of the Mississippi River. It also claimed a 140-acre amusement park, bringing to the city some of the best entertainment in the nation and attracting a national convention of editors. Within twenty years, the city had become one of the nation's leading livestock centers.

These achievements were created by outstanding leadership, beginning at the time of the Run of '89 and extending to the present. Such names as Henry and Ed Overholser, Charles Colcord, Mrs. Selwyn Douglas, C. G. Jones, Anton Classen, John Shartel, Dennis T. Flynn, and John and Peter Sinopoulo, to name just a few, were instrumental in its earlier days. But such leadership has continued over the years, including three generations of the Gaylord family, Stanley Draper Sr., and Stanley Draper, Jr., Fred Jones, Robert S. Kerr, Robert A. Hefner, George Shirk, Nan Sheets, Dean A. McGee, John and Eleanor Kirkpatrick, Harvey Everest, G. A. Nichols, Ray Ackerman, Bill Atkinson, Lee Allan Smith, and Jack Conn—again naming only a few examples.

The tragic and brutal bombing of 1995 will forever be a part of both local and national history. However, what we like to remember is not so much the bombing itself as the compassion of those in the community who came to the rescue in many ways, and those from throughout the nation who sent condolences, and in many cases, came to the city to volunteer assistance.

We hope you do not overlook the corporate and organizational histories in this volume. This is not only because the support of those organizations made this volume possible, but also because many of these organizational and personal histories are truly fascinating.

Among these stories you will read about a nationwide company started in a garage apartment; a highly technical company beginning after its founder failed an exam; a prestigious grocery founded in a tent shortly after the Run of '89; and two hospitals founded near the turn of the century.

You will also read about a highly sophisticated mass mailing company conceived by a twelve-year old boy sorting newspapers by hand, four companies which, collectively, have paved more than half the streets and highways in the county, and two of the oldest and most prestigious restaurants in Oklahoma County.

You will learn much about the entertainment history of the city and county through the story of two brothers who formed a 140-acre amusement park in the city shortly after the turn of the century. You will read of a man who, after retiring from both the Air Force and FAA, started a third career in his home as an aviation consultant, with clients now covering the nation.

In the area of public service, you will learn of the great work in health brought about by the Oklahoma Medical Research Foundation, and the contribution to youth—often troubled youth—performed by the Eagle Ridge Institute.

For your information, you can thank the following organizations as sponsors who made it possible for the Oklahoma City/County Historical Society to publish this history:

ACP Sheet Metal Company, Aero Tech Service, American Floral Services, Associated Communications and Research, Atlas Paving Company, Atlas Asphalt Products, Inc., Beam's Industries, Inc., Bishop Paving Company and Mega Supply Corporation, Cattlemen's Steakhouse, Crescent Market, Data Monitor Systems, Deaconess Hospital, Delong Mailing Company, Eagle Ridge Institute, Elaine Schuster, Goddard Concrete Company, Harry Mortgage Company, Kimray, Inc., the Lee family, Lincoln Plaza Hotel, Malcolm Hall Property Company, Materco, Inc., Matheny Concrete Products Company, McConnell Construction Inc., the Naifeh family, Oklahoma Medical Research Foundation, Presort First Class, Byron Gambulos, Sleepy Hollow, St. Anthony Hospital, Variety Health Center, and Zahl-Ford, Inc.

**Pendleton Woods**

*Boomers at the Kansas border in April 1889, getting ready to make the first land run.*

# CHAPTER I

## HOW THE TERRITORY CAME ABOUT

It can be said, almost without fear of contradiction, that Oklahoma has, not one, but the two most unique histories of any governmental entity in the world. Where else in the world is there a major area settled by forced removal of a race of people to that area? That marked the beginning of Indian Territory. And where else in the world is there a major area settled literally by a horse race? That is the beginning of Oklahoma Territory. Both histories also belong to Oklahoma County. Although present Oklahoma County was not occupied by the Indian tribes forced here, it was a part of the area given to the Creek and Seminole tribes in exchange for removal from the East. When the Run of 1889 took place, it was in the center of the land which became the first element of Oklahoma Territory.

Following the Revolutionary War and establishment of the United States, there was conflict west of the Mississippi River between Spain, which claimed the lands between the Mississippi River and the Rocky Mountains, and France, which had settled in some portions of the area, and

particularly New Orleans. After the turn of the eighteenth century, France, under Napoleon, held claim to these western lands, which it called Louisiana Territory. The French knew that they had only a shaky hold on this vast area of land, and were quickly ready to sell it at a bargain. It resulted in President Thomas Jefferson purchasing the entire area for $15 million in what still is recognized as the largest real estate deal in history.

At the same time there were movements in the United States to displace Indian tribes from the East. Lewis and Clark, Pike, Wilkinson and others explored the land and were convinced of its value. To the average American, it seemed like an endless frontier which would never be fully settled. Somewhere within this vast unsettled area, there must be a spot to remove the Indians, they rationalized. The area which is now Oklahoma was the most logical place. It was far enough west that, surely, it would never be settled otherwise. It was the southernmost area at the western extent of the territory, and principal eastern tribes were already in the south. The

movement of the Indian tribes began under President Andrew Jackson, in the 1830s.

When land was assigned to the tribes (often called nations), each was given territory extending almost to the Mexican border. Possessing, but not occupying the land which is now Oklahoma County were the Creek and Seminole Nations.

What was not anticipated was the American Civil War. Both the Northern and Southern governments were bidding for the support of the Indian Nations. For the most part, all five gave their allegiance to the Confederacy.

After the Civil War, as punishment to the tribes for aligning with the Confederacy, the Creek and Seminole Nations were required to sell back to the United States government an area more than two million acres for a price of $2 an acre. The Federal government intended to reassign this land to smaller tribes which were expected to be located in Indian Territory. This area—which eventually became Cleveland, Canadian, Logan, Payne, Oklahoma, and Kingfisher Counties—soon was known as the Unassigned Lands.

*Boomers adrift on the Canadian River.*

In the late 1870s movements were underway to force opening of the Unassigned Lands for settlement by homesteaders. In Congress there was opposition. Some wanted to move smaller Indian tribes into the area. Others wanted to use it for resettlement of Black freedmen. In 1879 the movement for white settlement was led by C. C. Carpenter, who gathered others interested in settlement and infiltrated the territory. Carpenter's strategy was to have wagons move into the territory, one wagon at a time. Eventually, he hoped, they would settle towns. Some individuals and businesses had invested money in those towns. President Rutherford B. Hayes ordered troops to the border to stop this infiltration, and eventually Carpenter's organization faded away.

David Payne followed Carpenter's experiment. Payne had homesteaded in Kansas and had served in the Fourth Kansas Infantry Regiment. When Carpenter's organization failed to achieve its goal, Captain Payne (as he was soon identified) became the leader of the movement. Under his command the effort became known as the Boomer Movement.

For five years, from late 1879 until his death at age forty-eight in 1884, Captain Payne was leader of the Boomers. His was a demonstration strategy. He would take large groups, sometimes nearly one hundred wagons at a time, into the territory. They knew they would be followed by cavalry. Usually they were simply returned to the border by the solders. On two occasions, however, Captain Payne was sent to Federal Court in Fort Smith, and once Payne was fined $1,000 (which he did not have) by Judge Isaac Parker. The strategy was to call attention to themselves and to their effort to settle the Unassigned Lands. The result was to gain additional Boomers and to slowly gain sympathy from some who had power in Washington. Thus, many were added to the Boomer movement.

One who joined was William L. Couch. He came to Kansas from North Carolina, and quickly became a principal lieutenant of David Payne. In the early 1880s, when Captain Payne's health was failing, Couch played an increasingly larger role in the effort. He took sizeable groups into the territory, often coming to the area which is now Oklahoma County. In 1884, after Captain Payne's death, Couch became the leader of the Boomers.

As the years passed, their leaders spent more and more time in Washington, lobbying with all who would listen to their argument for the opening of the territory. During the latter 1880s, sympathy was gradually changing toward settlement of the land. Railroads had become active in all five of the Indian Nations. There was increasing trade between Indians and Whites, and many of the Indians were becoming less hostile to white settlement.

The act of Congress which brought about the opening was actually a rider to the Indian Appropriation Bill in the final days of the administration of President Grover Cleveland. Cleveland was opposed to the rider, but he signed the bill. It was up to his successor, Benjamin Harrison, to carry out the terms of the rider, which called for the settlement of the Unassigned Lands within sixty days. Harrison selected what is

*The south corner of Grand (Sheridan) and Robinson on April 24, 1889, two days following the Run. Notice the jog in the roadway which resulted from competitive illegal surveys by different developers. This jog continued to exist for eighty years until it was corrected by the widening of the street west of the Myriad.*

probably the most unusual method ever used for the settlement of an area—a horse race from the borders of the Unassigned Lands directly into the area. The gun, signaling the start of the race, was set to be fired at noon, April 22, 1889. Thus, the development of what became Oklahoma County literally began with a bang.

There were six major townsites created by the Run of 1889. In addition to Oklahoma City, they included Guthrie, Norman, El Reno, Kingfisher, and Stillwater. The two largest were Guthrie and Oklahoma City. Also included might be Edmond, which was on the Santa Fe Railroad line, but it had only a hundred or so settlers. However, Edmond later grew to become one of the largest cities in Oklahoma.

Although the Run of 1889 is remembered in history as a horse race, those who settled Oklahoma City, for the most part, didn't arrive by horse. Instead they came by the Santa Fe Railroad, which was not allowed to travel any faster than a horse could run. The Santa Fe had reached what was later Oklahoma City in 1887, moving southward toward Texas. A station was built to the north of the North Canadian River. Called Oklahoma Station, it would later become Oklahoma City. It is no accident that Oklahoma City was to be located at its present location. The two principal needs for a community location then—and now—are transportation and water. At that time, railroads were the only means of transportation, other than animals, and thus the spot where the only rail line in the territory crossed the North Canadian River was a natural location for a townsite.

Just how many people made the Run of '89 will never be known. No one made a count. Even if they had totaled the number at every border, the result still would not have been accurate. Thousands had slipped in earlier as "sooners," hiding among the creek beds, in the underbrush and wherever they could not be seen. In this manner they could appear at their pre-determined claim ahead of those who

G. A. Beidler, the first Oklahoma City postmaster following the Run of 1889, is pictured at his post office at #8 West Street.

Frank Harrah's Pioneer Restaurant operated out of a tent during the period immediately following the Run of 1889.

obeyed the law and waited for the signal to start the race. Estimates of the number making the run vary from 25,000 to 50,000 or more. Neither is it known how many came to Oklahoma County. Low estimates range from 5,000 to 6000, but the estimate of Captain David F. Stiles, provost marshal at Oklahoma station, was that the first day's crowd ranged between 10,000 and 13,000 persons. By the time the first census was taken, many had left and others had moved in. It can truly be said, however, that Oklahoma City is one of the few cities in the world to be "born grown," moving from virtually zero population to approximately ten thousand in a single day.

Oklahoma City, from the beginning, was destined to be a principal city, if not the principal city of what would some day be the state of Oklahoma, since it was at the crossing of a river by the only railroad line in the area. At the time of the opening, six frame buildings were already in existence—a depot, the home of the station agent, a section house, a shack to serve as a

*Western National Bank was established on the northwest corner of Main and Broadway in Oklahoma City in the mid-1890s.*

*The First Methodist Church at Northwest Fourth and Robinson at a time when the area was primarily residential. The church is the only church in Oklahoma City at the exact location of its first 1889 worship service. Badly damaged by the 1995 bombing, its has been restored and enlarged, retaining its original style and beauty.*

post office, a government office structure, and the stockade of the stage line which passed through the area. Town promoters knew of these advantages, and they came to Oklahoma Station with town lots platted and ready to sell to those who arrived.

Although the promoters did not own the lots, and certainly had no authority to sell them, most prospective settlers realized that if they did not pay the $25, or whatever a lot cost, they would lose to somebody who did.

To make matters worse, there were actually two companies developing the projected city. The Seminole Land and Improvement Company (not related to the Seminole Indian Nation) was surveying and marking streets north of the street named for its leading promoter, Sidney Clarke (Clarke Street later became known as Grand Avenue, and is now Sheridan Avenue). The Oklahoma Colony Company set up a huge headquarters tent where the American National Bank later stood and proclaimed its town to be South Oklahoma, south of Grand Avenue.

The federal government had made no provisions for city lots, streets or alleys. This resulted in a great amount of turbulence, with fights, lot jumping, illegal sales, and hasty confusion. To add to the confusion, the Seminole development company surveyed westward from the dirt roadway west of the railroad tracks, while the Oklahoma Colony Company surveyed directly from the tracks. Thus the surveys of the two land companies did not match. This created a jog wherever a north-south street crossed Clarke. The purpose of a "Committee of 13," elected three days after the Run, and which, in effect, was the new community's first city council, was to straighten out the surveys and eliminate the jogs. However, the effort failed, and it was not until more than one hundred years later after a period of urban renewal, the building of the Myriad and the Myriad Gardens, and the widening of Hudson and Walker, that the jog was finally eliminated.

The conduct of the first election in Oklahoma City was almost as unusual as the run itself. The men who settled the town came from all parts of the nation. In general, the people of the new town did not know one another. Angelo Scott, a twenty-one-year-old man who later formed the first newspaper in the town, and who still later would become president of Territorial Oklahoma A&M College, was elected chairman of the town meeting. He attributed his selection to his clear, resonant voice, which could easily be heard and understood. Whenever someone was nominated, the cry of the public was: "Let's see him." He was then shoved onto the platform to the chairman's side, and questioned by the multitude. If they liked his looks, they voted him up. If not, they voted him down. This procedure was continued until thirteen persons were elected to the committee.

At a later election, about a month afterward, a provisional mayor and council were elected. It was considered provisional because there was no legislation for government in the bill which created the Run. The settlers, in fact, had no laws except for those they created unofficially for themselves. William Couch, who had long been leader of the Boomer Movement, was elected mayor. He was already at Oklahoma Station at the time of the Run, but he was not a Sooner. Couch was an employee of the Santa Fe Railroad. He thought that in this position he could claim land, which he did, west of Oklahoma City. But there was another claimant and a dispute. As result of this dispute, Coach was wounded the following Spring and died shortly

*A view of Oklahoma City four weeks after the Run of 1889.*

afterwards from the wound. Like Moses who led the movement to the Promised Land, William Couch, the man who had perhaps worked hardest for the opening of the Unassigned Lands, did not live to enjoy owning land in the new territory.

In the months following the run, the town was bounded by the Santa Fe railway, Northwest Seventh Street, Walker, and Southwest Seventh Street. As for population, a survey made on June 14, 1889, reported 2,685 men, 721 women,

and 736 children, for a total of 4,138. Although it is known that many who made the run had moved away during the first two months, this survey, if at all accurate, tended to support a lower number of original settlers than the ten thousand estimated by Captain Stiles.

The survey also showed that there were 1,602 occupied dwellings, three water wells, no street surfacing, no sewers, no permanent sidewalks, and no parks. There were 34 grocery stories, 21 drug stores, 15 meat markets, 5 furniture stores, 37 restaurants, 10 hotels, 20 boarding houses, 14 barber shops, 4 banks (with deposits of $120,000), 29 real estate firms, 53 doctors, 2 dentists, 5 newspapers, 7 ice cream parlors, 11 laundries, 6 livery stables, and 11 flour and feed stores. Some of these establishments were only what the proprietors said they were and some of the "establishments" were almost of a handcart variety.

Less than a month after the opening, a Board of Trade was formed. This board, the predecessor to the Oklahoma City Chamber of Commerce, has, more than any other organization or elected group, dominated growth, development and policies of the city. Henry Overholser was the board's first president. Although location played the principal role in Oklahoma City being one of the largest

*The first Oklahoma City grocery store, established in a tent on April 22, 1889.*

*An Oklahoma City street scene from 1890.*

original settlements, it was leadership and vision which vaulted it forward after the tents were replaced with wooden shacks. Much of this leadership came from Henry Overholser, although he failed in his try for mayor of the city which he helped so much.

While some pioneer communities thought in terms of one-story wooden buildings, Henry Overholser was thinking in terms of multi-stories. Within a few months after the Run he brought in six pre-fabricated, two story buildings, all alike, which were placed side by side, extending west from the northwest corner of Grand and Robinson. They remained there until 1908. Diagonally across the street, he constructed a frame building and placed Oklahoma City's first opera house on the second floor. This auditorium, makeshift by today's standards, became the principal place for social events as well as stage entertainment. Two law offices, also on the second floor, served as dressing rooms for plays and other entertainment, where changing of costumes was required.

Government in the first year following the Run could only be described as "provisional," and the first city officials as "provisional officers." This was because,

in the haste to open the land within the sixty days which the Congressional rider prescribed, a territory had not been created by Congress. Actually, it was on May 2, 1890—more than one year after the opening of the Unassigned Lands— that Congress got around to creating Oklahoma Territory, establishing rules of government, selecting a territorial capital, and naming a territorial governor. Thus, Oklahoma County was not created until

1890, along with the other five counties. Oklahoma City and Edmond, which was beginning to grow, were the principal communities of Oklahoma County. Guthrie, in Logan County, was designated by Congress to become the capital of Oklahoma Territory.

Almost immediately there was a struggle by other communities of the territory—principally Oklahoma City and Kingfisher—to get the territorial capital designation. At one time Oklahoma City and Kingfisher agreed that if one of them did not get the capital, it would throw its support to the other. Several times after the territorial capital was created, there were proposals in the territorial legislature for removing the capital to a different location, and sometimes a vote was prohibited by political maneuvering. In order to soften the effort, other communities were given the locations of the first colleges. Norman was given the territorial college, which became the University of Oklahoma. Stillwater was given the agricultural and mechanical college, now Oklahoma State University. Edmond, which was beginning to grow, was given the normal (teachers) college, which is now the University of Central Oklahoma.

*Robinson Street looking north from Grand about the turn of the century. At left is one of six prefabricated buildings brought to the new city by Henry Overholser in 1889. These buildings came down in 1908, and the Colcord Building was built on the corner.*

*The arrival of the morning train at the Santa Fe Station on July 4, 1890.*

# Chapter II

## OKLAHOMA TERRITORIAL DAYS

Oklahoma City was practically under military rule for nine months. Captain David Stiles of the Tenth U.S. Infantry, which had been stationed at Fort Reno, served as provost marshal. Captain Stiles had a difficult time, since there were no laws in effect except those of the federal government. There was only one railway—the Santa Fe—entering Oklahoma City on the day of its settlement. The Choctaw (later to become the Rock Island) was approaching from the east, but at the time of the Run was only about halfway to Oklahoma City from the Arkansas border.

A common school system had to be set up for Oklahoma Territory at the beginning of the Territorial period. A lavish Congress had given $50,000 for the temporary support for common schools. It was decided that there should be four schools for each township and that a high school for each township (or city over five hundred) provided that no high school be maintained unless common schools were first provided. Sections 16 and 36 of each township were set aside for supporting elementary and secondary schools.

An important event in the fall of 1890 was the opening of the Overholser Opera House. On November 29, 1890, John Dillon

appeared in *Wanted: The Earth*. The first New Year's reception was January 1, 1891, hosted by Captain and Mrs. Stiles, whose home was on the military reservation east of the tracks, later known as the Maywood addition. The first music club to be organized in Oklahoma County was the Philharmonic in 1892, with A. C. Scott as president. Its purpose was to stimulate interest in things musical and to present choral work. During the first four years parts of Handel's *Messiah* and *The Creation* were given together with a number of concerts.

In 1890 Oklahoma City was second in size of the four major communities opened by the Run. Guthrie was by far the largest, and Kingfisher was somewhat behind Oklahoma City. Within a month after its birth, Oklahoma City had as many as thirty business structures other than tents. Ten of these were two stories and eight belonged to Henry Overholser. They were substantial, durable business houses and were plastered. These were the first privately owned structures in the territory to be so treated. This was the first step in the physical superiority of Oklahoma City over her rivals. It was Overholser's business daring which had the effect of enthusing others to build substantial buildings, and at

the end of a year after its birth, commerce had gained greatly. In June 1890 county government was organized.

What was believed to be the first oil drilling adventure in Oklahoma Territory was started with a prayer picnic and a picture of new wells. Oklahoma City was not a year old when a wildcatter started an oil test at the intersection of Fourth Street and the Santa Fe tracks, then out on the edge of a growing town. Drilling started in the spring of 1890. A basket picnic was held, and the minister blessed the tools and the drillers. Drilling proceeded haphazardly during the year, and the next spring the well was abandoned at about six hundred feet.

No one was born for the first nine days after Oklahoma Territory was settled, but on May 1, 1889, a daughter was born to Mr. and Mrs. J. W. Cunningham, whom they named Oklahoma Belle. Years later, after marriage, her name was Oklahoma Belle Cheever. For many years afterwards the name was recognized in Oklahoma City as Cheever's Flowers, a store founded by her family.

One of the first necessities of a civilization is a jail. A crude one was erected immediately after Oklahoma City officers were elected. While the city had a jail before a church, there was still no lack of religious services.

HISTORICAL ROUTE 66

*The Round Barn of Arcadia, constructed in 1898 and restored in the early 1990s.*

The first Sunday after the Run, church services were held in at least three places. At the well at the intersection of Main and Broadway, Reverend C. C. Hembree, formerly of Kansas City, stationed himself and opened a service after the Presbyterian Church style. A large crowd gathered about him. About three blocks to the north, W. P. Shaw, a layman, conducted a Sunday School under the auspices of the South Methodist Church. It resulted in the First Methodist Episcopal Church South, now known as St. Luke's United Methodist Church.

The Southern Baptists began their work in Oklahoma City a short time after the Run. In July a meeting was called to consider organization of a Baptist Church with more than thirty names given the first week. Early preaching was by W. H. Nichols.

Catholics in Oklahoma City formed the St. Joseph's parish on April 23, 1889—only one day after the Run. The First St. Joseph's church at Northwest Fourth and Harvey, was dedicated less than two weeks later. The first service of the First Christian Church, Disciples of Christ, in Oklahoma City was held at what is now the intersection of Main and Broadway in the open air. Sixteen persons were enrolled and made up the charter members. After this first Sunday, the

church met in a small frame building near First and Robinson, and afterwards had a frame building at the northwest corner of First and Harvey. Pilgrim Congregational Church was another of the early denominations organized during the year of the Run of 1889, worshipping initially in the parlor of Mrs. Brown's Boarding House at the northwest corner of Hudson and California.

When Oklahoma Territory was formed, it included the area covered by the six counties which made up the former Unassigned Lands—Oklahoma, Canadian, Cleveland, Noble, Payne, and Kingfisher. It also included the Panhandle of Oklahoma, separated geographically from the six counties. This area was identified as Cimarron Territory, but was often called "No Man's Land." George W. Steele was appointed territorial governor by President Harrison. In 1890 Governor Steele reported to the secretary of the Interior, a condition of confusion. Although the six county seats had been established—Stillwater, Guthrie, Oklahoma City, Norman, Kingfisher, and El Reno—county boundaries had not been defined. The governor had to do this and then take an enumeration as the basis for representation in the first legislature. Logan County led in population by 14,254,

followed by Oklahoma County with 12,794. Of the other county seats, Kingfisher had 1,258, Norman had 764, Stillwater had 615, and El Reno had 519. Every quarter-section of land opened to settlement was occupied. In many instances there were two settlers claiming the same quarter and as many as five upon a quarter in some instances. When President Harrison signed the Organic Act, creating the territory, Governor Steele conducted the first Federal census and set election for members of the first Territorial Legislature for July 8.

Even before the territory was formally organized as a body, political parties had been formed. Twice in the summer of 1889, Guthrie had called conventions in the hope of calling off Oklahoma City's intentions on becoming the capital, but they had failed. A Republican Territorial Convention was held at Oklahoma City January 17, 1890, with 150 delegates present. It made no endorsements, but paved the way for a central committee meeting a month later at Frisco, Oklahoma, where an organization was perfected. Frisco is in the area now occupied by Yukon.

George Gardenhire, the lone Populist in the group, was elected president of the council (Senate) for the first legislature. He came out of it with A&M College for his own tiny city of Stillwater. Edmond got a state normal (teachers) school. Norman got the territorial university.

As a result of the trading, Oklahoma City won the designation of territorial capital. However, Governor Steele vetoed the bill at Guthrie's urging, and perhaps after consultation with President Harrison.

Determined to punish Guthrie, Oklahoma City then swung its forces to Kingfisher for the capital, but again Governor Steele vetoed the action and saved the day for Guthrie. Kingfisher was without sufficient support in the legislature to win the designation for itself.

Guthrie's most capable leader in the capital fight was William H. Merten, a member of the House. He was skilled in parliamentary procedure. He believed that Oklahoma City had received money from

Kingfisher in Kingfisher's efforts to get the capital. And if this were true he didn't believe that Oklahoma City would desert Kingfisher. So Merten prepared a substitute bill to be offered in place of the Kingfisher bill. The assembly became a mob, pistols were drawn, and men shook pistols in each others' faces. The sergeant at arms was ordered to clear the House. Brown took the floor again when the floor was cleared, but was knocked down. The railroads also entered the capital fight. The Santa Fe railroad and the Choctaw (later the Rock Island) were in conflict throughout the removal fight. The Santa Fe, which served both Guthrie and Oklahoma City, was determined to hold the capital on its line. The Rock Island, which was moving toward Oklahoma City, but would not go to Guthrie, was fighting to make the capital in Oklahoma City.

Actually the first legislative session gave so much attention to locating the capital, it had only ten days in which to pass a code of laws for the territory. Those laws, in the main, were taken from the statutes of several states. To get votes for the capital, both Oklahoma City and Guthrie promised to locate institutions in cities which would aid them in the capital fight.

The capital fight remained an important part of Oklahoma City history throughout the Territorial period and into statehood. In the first county elections, the Democrats and Populists made a clean sweep, and it was nearly an even break in the legislature. The Democrats charged that the Republicans had campaigned while taking the census. It was also charged that they had gerrymandered their districts in their own interest. In September 1890, just after the first legislature met, the voters elected a Republican, Judge D. A. Harvey of Oklahoma City, as delegate to Congress (non-voting). Democrats and Populists had been unable to agree on a fusion candidate.

In establishing institutions, the legislature required the three cities receiving colleges—Stillwater, Edmond and Norman—to vote $5,000 in bonds for the buildings. Norman and Edmond provided 40 acres, of which 30 were sold

to secure building funds. Stillwater had to guarantee an entire 160 acres for the agricultural college. Also the first legislature provided for farming out of its convicts to Kansas and its insane to Illinois.

The first needs for any new city are utilities. Although the first working electric light had been created by Thomas Edison barely over ten years earlier, the brand new Oklahoma City was going after electricity.

C. G. Jones (after whom the community of Jones in Oklahoma County was later named) operated a gristmill on the North Canadian River in south Oklahoma City. He took the lead in promoting electric service to Oklahoma City through a proposed water-powered generator on the Canadian River near his mill. The people of Oklahoma City were enthusiastic, and those in the business community were quick to shell out their hard-earned money to invest in such a venture. The plant was scheduled to go on the line at the close of 1890, and people gathered with excitement to see the beginning of an electric system, which would initially light up downtown. Water was released to turn the turbines. There was a flicker of light, but water at the dam began to sink into the sand. It was soon learned that the venture was a failure. There was disappointment in loss of investment, but even more disappointment that the awaited

lighting of downtown was not to be—at least for the present. However, it was not long before a Colorado company came in with a small steam generator. Over the first ten years of Territorial Oklahoma City, several different companies became involved, but in 1902, electric properties were purchased by a fledgling company—the Oklahoma Gas and Electric Company.

Early in 1890 a contract was made with the Oklahoma Ditch and Canal Company and J. F. Thompson of Houston to provide a system of water works. However, it seemed to city officials that Thompson was merely speculating in the enterprise, because as late as mid-1892 he was still inactive and the town was in dire need of good water. Eventually, General Henry G. Thomas of Maine appeared and, after looking things over, bought the water works and developed a system which would serve the community in its early years.

W. J. Gault, a prominent lumberman, was nominated and elected mayor of Oklahoma City under the new Territorial laws of 1890. At the first meeting the council leased a two story brick building with a basement at 13 North Broadway at the rental of $25 per month. A wholesale liquor dealer was on the first floor, and above it were the city offices, police headquarters and police court. The city jail was in the basement. The Roberts

*The Threadgill Hotel was the first major hotel to open in downtown Oklahoma City following the Run.*

Hotel later occupied the site of this structure.

Gault led in the granting of a franchise to the Choctaw Coal and Railway Company (later the Rock Island) for an east-west railway through the city. In 1889 there had been conflicting claims between the Choctaw Company and Oklahoma City land claimers who had staked lots on the right-of-way on the day of the land opening. A compromise came about, with the right-of-way being reduced.

the political fight ended shortly after the Organic Act of May 1890 because Territorial Governor Steele, in designating counties, ordered that Oklahoma City and South Oklahoma be incorporated together as the Village of Oklahoma City.

Two dominating figures in the progress of early Oklahoma City were C. G. Jones and Henry Overholser. Jones was not as highly literate in his speech as some of the leaders, but he had a most persuasive

in and sending on the Frisco, he was the prime figure in establishing the railroad facilities which were absolutely necessary in order to establish Oklahoma City as the distribution point of a vast territory. He was twice mayor of Oklahoma City. He was a member of the first territorial legislature and the first state legislature. He was a leader for statehood and, after that, a force in bringing the capital to Oklahoma City. He died just prior to World War I.

Henry Overholser was the leading original builder in Oklahoma City. He and his son, Ed, came to the city with wealth enough to bring six prefabricated two story frame business buildings, which extended west from Robinson on Clarke Street (later Grand and now Sheridan). In 1890 he built the first Overholser Opera House on the southeast corner of Clarke and Robinson, replaced ten years later by a much more imposing building in the adjoining block to the west. His imposing home at Northwest Fifteenth and Hudson is now a historic show home operated by the Oklahoma Historical Society.

His son, Ed, was mayor of Oklahoma City in the World War I era and oversaw the construction of the city's first reservoir lake, named in his honor.

*The Fairchild Winery, constructed in 1892, was used for commercial production of wine until statehood brought Prohibition in 1907.*

There was also trouble in South Oklahoma, which had started as a separate municipality, and which was laid off on the second day. Officers for South Oklahoma were elected, with G. W. Patrick being its first mayor. An ordinance was quickly passed, providing for occupation taxes and payment for lot certificates. This quickly became a sensitive subject. Charges of corruption were made and indignation meetings were held. Patrick resigned under pressure in less than a month and the treasurer, who had failed to make bond, disappeared. A South Oklahoma charter agitation started, and under the south Oklahoma charter, another election was held, with T. J. Fagen being elected mayor. Troubles grew, and soon a movement was on to impeach Mayor Fagen. The mayor headed this off by resigning. In April, 1890 another election was held under the charter. However,

power through his enthusiasm and his sales ability. Jones was the promoter and builder of railroads from the first. He presided at a meeting concerning the Choctaw right-of-way. Later he took up the matter of extending the Frisco railroad from Sapulpa to Oklahoma City and organized the St. Louis and Oklahoma City Railroad Company. Then he turned his eyes to the southwest. He organized the Oklahoma City Southwestern and built to Quanah, Texas, serving Chickasha, Lawton, Snyder, and other towns. This also became part of the Frisco. He built another line, which was absorbed by the Frisco, from Red Fork through Pawnee, Perry, and Enid to Avard.

Jones organized a company which built a line seventy miles, running from Chandler to Okmulgee. Thus, by helping to secure the Choctaw (Rock Island) and by bringing

During the years 1891-1892 an effort was made to establish a school fund in Oklahoma City. Sidney Clarke went to Washington to represent the school system, trying to get the former military area granted for school purposes. This reservation had not been in use after Oklahoma was opened to settlement. It was just east of the original Oklahoma City boundary and covered 160 acres. It extended to Durland Avenue on the east, Reno on the south, and the Santa Fe tracks on the west. Clarke and Captain David Stiles worked to get this bill passed in Congress in 1892 and failed. The following winter they returned to Washington, along with Dennis T. Flynn, the territorial delegate to Congress. They placed it before the committee on public lands and the bill became a law in the session of 1894.

In the first county election in 1891 an unexpected entry was the Women's

Christian Temperance Union, which drafted an address to the voters, published in the Gazette. They took a firm stand against intemperance and soonerisms.

Oklahoma's own underworld became a threat during the early 1890s because of the tie of politics and business with the underworld. It was hard to crush this threat. Many businessmen and newspapers not only defended, but actually fought for a wide open town. Many big time gamblers, haughty madams, and arrogant saloon keepers told politicians and public officials what to do and when to do it. This tough element was basically in the block of ground from Broadway to Front Street and Grand Avenue and California, the site of the present-day Myriad. This area was referred to as "Hell's Half Acre". It covered an entire block, but the vilest part was Hop Boulevard, which was just back of the Bastille de Cottonwood (first jail), where the notorious Southern Club was later built. Possibly the worst resort was the Red Onion, presided over by the Madame Daisy Clayton.

There was much building in early Oklahoma City. Fifty-two days after the opening, Oklahoma City had 1,603 occupied houses and 570 places of business, and by June 1 lots on Main Street were selling at prices ranging from $100 to $1,000. The city was less than one month old when the its board of trade (later chamber of commerce) was organized with twenty-one directors

The second territorial legislature in 1892 inserted a provision in the legislative reapportionment bill saying "provided further that the legislative assembly elected under this act shall not consider any proposition or pass any bills to remove the seat of government of the said territory from its present location." This same provision was in the appropriation bills of 1894, 1896, and 1898.

The Congressional prohibition on the territorial capital said nothing about the location of public buildings. A council member from Enid (entering the Territory through the Run of 1893) became leader of a combine to locate public institutions. Guthrie at first did not want anything to do with the combine, but later became

*The Hotel Lee, built on the southeast corner of Main and Broadway in the early 1890s, was destroyed by fire a few years later. It was replaced by the Lee-Huckins Hotel at the same location.*

involved. Oklahoma City wanted the capital and was against the scheme. This combine was aimed at securing buildings for Oklahoma Territory which later might go to Indian Territory following joint statehood. Friends of the combine became known as the "mound builders," and its opponents were called the "cave dwellers". In its final form, the bill appropriated $100,000 for a law library building in Guthrie, to become a nucleus of the capitol. Benefiting from the bill were Enid, El Reno, Kingfisher, Ponca City, Alva, Langston, Stillwater, Norman, Tonkawa, and Edmond. The Guthrie location was not inserted until the bill reached the House. It was said that Oklahoma City made the suggestion that brought the amendment in the House for the $100,000 building. The amendment was rejected in the council and finally struck from the bill. Governor Barnes vetoed the bill because of its excessive appropriation and because of the methods employed in its passage. Congress plugged the rat hole by forbidding the Territorial Legislature to make any appropriations or to enter into any contacts for public buildings. This was enforced until the time of statehood.

The Women's Christian Temperance Union started a crusade for prohibition,

which culminated seventeen years later in the state constitution. In 1893 Reverend Sam Small, a nationally known evangelist, politician, and editor from Atlanta, Georgia, opened a three-week revival in the First Baptist Church. It was an appeal for Oklahoma City to do something about its dens of iniquity. He was himself a reformed drunkard. His sermon drew a large crowd, and was considered to be a great success.

It was announced that he had decided to hang his hat in Oklahoma City and to establish a daily newspaper, which would be called the *Daily Oklahoman*. It would have two objectives—single statehood (excluding Indian Territory) and constitutional prohibition. The first issue of the *Daily Oklahoman* appeared January 14, 1894, which was a Sunday morning. There was considerable criticism about a minister putting his first paper out on a Sunday, but the paper was well received. The Small venture in Oklahoma City failed because businessmen held the purse strings in advertising. They would not stand for moral crusades against the saloons, which were a part of the city's commercial life.

The year 1893 brought about the founding of an organization in Kingfisher by the Oklahoma Territorial Press Association, which later became known as the Oklahoma Historical Society. Formed under the leadership of William Campbell, its original purpose was to collect, arrange and preserve all newspapers, magazines and books published in Oklahoma. The collections of this organization later moved to Norman, then, after the turn of the century, were moved to the upper floor of the new Carnegie Library in Oklahoma City. When the Capitol building was constructed, the collections were moved there. This led eventually to the building of the Oklahoma Historical Society structure in the State Capitol complex in 1929.

Oklahoma City went through its greatest financial crisis in July 1893, when two of the city's three banks failed. There was a run, which lasted long after banking hours, on the third institution, which was the First National Bank. Oklahoma City then had a population of about five thousand, and with the panic of 1893 in full swing, cash was scarce. Officers of the three banks had been fearing a run for weeks.

About 11 a.m., July 19, James H. Wheeler, cashier of the bank on the southwest corner of Grand and Robinson, stepped outside the bank and nailed a notice to the door that the bank was insolvent and closed. News spread like a prairie fire through the town. In a few minutes lines had formed at the First National Bank on the southwest corner of Main and Broadway and the Oklahoma National Bank across the street to its east, where the Huckins Hotel later stood. The Oklahoma National, which was the outgrowth of the old Citizens Bank, soon was forced to close its doors. However, the First National, which had shipped in a big supply of cash for reserve, continued to pay its customers in full all day and into the night.

Men fought for a place in the long line and cashiers continued to check each account carefully and hand over the total in cash. Finally T. M. Richardson, president of the bank, manned the front steps, and held up his hand for a signal of silence. "We are closing now," he said. "We figure twelve hours is a good banking day. We will be open

in the morning, and all of you who have not been waited on can have your money if you want it. But I want to tell you, there is enough money to pay off every depositor, and if any man loses a dollar, I want to be hanged to that telephone pole over there."

As a matter of fact, cash was running low. But as Richardson made his talk, a number of employees of the bank arrived and carried full money sacks into the bank while the crowd looked on. The sacks were filled with washers. That night, M. L. Turner and Joe McNeil, bankers of Guthrie, drove to Oklahoma City with more cash to save the First National Bank. However, when morning came, a line was formed outside with depositors anxious to get their money back into the bank again.

Started in 1894 and completed in 1895, the Washington and Emerson Schools were the first schools in Oklahoma City to be erected. They were occupied after the Christmas holidays in 1895. Soon afterwards a high school was built and, later, was enlarged. This was the Irving School, later the Webster School, and then was used as a black school. Later the Bryant, Lincoln, Jefferson, McKinley, and Garfield Schools were built. In 1909 four other schools were under construction, including a new high school, later known as Central High.

One of Oklahoma City's worst tragedies was the killing of the chief of police Milton Jones on June 30, 1895, after the jail break by three notorious outlaws—Jim Casey and Bob and Bill Christian. All were being held in county jail on convictions of murder. The Oklahoma County jail was then a two-story wooden structure with two steel cages on the first floor. The jail was located at an alley north of Grand Avenue between Broadway and Robinson. Those alleys had been given the names of Wall Street and Maiden Lane.

The first library association, headed by Mrs. Selwyn Douglas, started a small library in 1895. The books had no home and almost no shelves. Mrs. Douglas wrote Andrew Carnegie asking him to build a library for Oklahoma City. Carnegie replied that if Oklahoma City would spend $2,000

a year maintaining the library and would furnish the site, he would pay the expense of building a structure up to the cost of $25,000. This was in 1899. The women raised the money to buy the grounds of the library, and in forty-eight hours they got the subscriptions for $1,750 to purchase the four lots on which the library was located. By the time of Statehood, the library had eight thousand books. In honor of Mrs. Douglas, a memorial bronze fountain, known as the Douglas Memorial Fountain, was placed on the grounds.

By 1895 the finances of the county were at a low state. County warrants sold for forty cents on the dollar. Earlier, in 1894, Ed Overholser, son of Henry Overholser was commissioner of Oklahoma County. He instructed the treasurer to pay no more warrants because he needed funds for operating current affairs. When warrants were presented, the treasurer sent the owner to Overholser and the owner was indignant. Overholser told the owners that the county had an attorney, hired for the year, and could defend lawsuits at small cost. Then he outlined the plan to appease the holder. He held off the creditors until he could get a bill through the legislature refunding all outstanding warrants. Thus in a day, Overholser put Oklahoma County on a cash basis, and that fall he reduced the levy almost in half.

Oklahoma City was also growing in size physically. The original townsite had been full since the first day. South Oklahoma City had earlier become an addition to Oklahoma City. The military reservation, with 160 acres on the east side, had been added by an act of Congress, through the efforts of Dennis Flynn.

About 1896 George W. Massey had opened a quarter section east and north of town, and named it Maywood, in honor of his daughter. Then came the Gault 80 acres, lying just north of Seventh Street. The Gault 80 plat was filled by 1898. In April 1901 Owen and Welch bought and platted the Higgins quarter lying just west of town. This was the original Couch claim and the old courthouse stood upon it.

*The interior of an unidentified Oklahoma City downtown store, c. 1903.*

# CHAPTER III

## A NEW CENTURY BEGINS

Oklahoma City began its new century with a great deal of optimism. It showed a population of 14,369 people. It had a new city hall ready to be occupied. The Carnegie Library was completed. Building operations for the year totaled $1.2 million and there were contracts for the next year. The new Stiles Park in the near northeast part of the city was dedicated. The Frisco Railroad line had arrived in the city. The city had a $45,000 sewer system, ample for future growth. The post office was handling twice the volume of business it had handled four years earlier.

The first year of the century was a major year for street improvements. Sidewalks were being laid. During a single three-month period there was laid an 18,179 foot boardwalk, 1,225 feet of stone walk, 4,150 feet of cement walk, and 550 feet of asphalt walk.

Land was purchased for a new central fire station, and the force of paid firemen was set to be increased. In 1900 the total number of fire runs for the year was forty-four, with total damage of $3,305. Principal expenses of the fire department for the year were $2,147 for salaries of regular firemen and $90 for volunteer firemen. Other costs included feeding horses, $96.70; shoeing horses, $15.10; drugs and veterinary services, $21.75; hiring extra horses, $4; and extra wagons, $42.

Stiles Park, given to the city by Captain Stiles, was the beginning of a park system for Oklahoma City. In the 1890s there were neither public or private parks. Gatherings were held in Durland's Wood or McClure's Grove, where there were stretches of natural timber. When the Maywood addition in northeast Oklahoma City was platted, there was a small circular park. For about five years

Stiles Park was a source of annoyance to the Oklahoma City Council because of people wanting to spend a few dollars to improve it. Money was scarce, and it was hard to get money to maintain parks. However, in 1902, banker James B. Wheeler proposed to give the city a piece of woodland along the river at the southwest city limits. The only stipulation called for an appropriation of city funds of not less than $2,000 per year to improve and maintain it. The council had to almost be forced to accept the gift. Wheeler Park, early in its history, was the home of the only zoological garden in the state. Donations of rare animals came fast, but the board was without funds to provide cages, and had to resort to make-shift quarters. By 1920 the zoo contained more than 125 specimens, ranging from bear to seals to monkeys and badgers, in addition to a fine collection of birds.

*Boating at Putnam Park in 1909. Putnam Park was located between Classen and Western, south of Northwest Thirty-sixth Street on land given to the city by I. M. Putnam. The park is now known as Memorial Park.*

The Arkansas Valley Telephone Company, which had served Oklahoma City, had its name changed to Pioneer Telephone Company in 1902, and fifteen years later it became Southwestern Bell.

Oklahoma City took a giant step forward in entertainment when two Greek immigrant brothers—John and Peter Sinopoulo—came from St. Louis to organize a 140-acre amusement park, which they named Delmar Garden. Extending south and west from about Western and Reno, this park included a restaurant and beer garden, the Delmar Theater for vaudeville and concerts, a race track, a stage for events, thrill rides, and numerous other items of entertainment. It brought the finest events to Oklahoma City. *Dan Patch*, the most famous race horse of its time, raced there. The daring Barney Oldfield burned the auto race track at sixty miles per hour. Geronimo would be released from prison in Fort Sill to sign autographs at Delmar for ten cents each. The National Editorial Convention, along with other meetings and conventions, was held there. Delmar was the place to go in Oklahoma City until it closed at the end of the 1909 season.

Another major entertainment addition to the city was the second Overholser Opera House, built by Henry Overholser on the north side of Grand Avenue between Robinson and Harvey. It replaced a wooden structure which Overholser had constructed at Grand and Robinson in 1890. The Overholser was the premier playhouse of Oklahoma at that time and for some time to come. It had the largest stage west of the Mississippi River—even larger than the opera house in St. Louis. As many as fifty people at one time have appeared on the stage. It brought to Oklahoma City some of the finest concerts and vaudeville productions in the nation. In the early 1920s it became the Orpheum Theater, bringing attractions of the Orpheum circuit, and in its latter years it was the Warner Theater. Other early theaters were the State, the Empire, and the Bijou Theaters, all of which began with high-class vaudeville in the first years of the century.

The City Hall, completed in 1902 at the corner of Broadway and Grand, was three stories high with a basement used by the police department. Portions of the second and third story were rented out, which produced revenue to retire a bond issue.

The biggest fire in early days in the city was in 1903, when the Lion Store at Main and Robinson burned, and threatened to wipe out the entire city. Fire departments came from Guthrie, El Reno and Purcell to assist.

This was also the year for the first streetcars. It was on February 2, 1903, that most of Oklahoma City's population crowded downtown for an inspiring celebration, and to see the first streetcar in either Oklahoma or Indian Territory move over the newly laid tracks. W. W. Storm and John Shartel were principals in this venture.

In 1904 the Oklahoma conferences of the Methodist Episcopal Church and the Methodist Episcopal Church South voted to unite and establish a university in Oklahoma, to be located on a spacious campus west of the present-day Classen High School. The land for the campus was donated by Anton Classen. Buildings were erected, and, in September 1904, Epworth University was opened under joint management of the two churches. Shortly afterwards, they formed a medical and dental school, with intern and resident practice being at St. Anthony and Rolater Hospitals. After about three years the medical and dental schools were closed and passed to the University of Oklahoma. The university closed in 1911, when the two church bodies

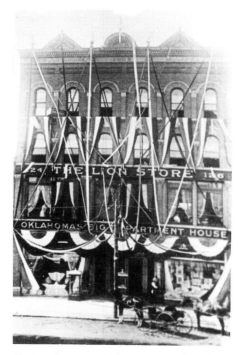

*The Lion Store, an early department store located near Grand and Broadway, is decorated to welcome the National Editorial Convention, held in the city in 1905.*

decided that each should maintain its own educational facilities. In many ways, Epworth was the forerunner of Oklahoma City University. The present day Epworth Methodist Church occupies the administration building of the former Epworth University.

The Weather Bureau took over the site at the southwest corner of Northwest Nineteenth and Classen for its headquarters. It bought the site from Epworth University for $10.

Another educational institution, long forgotten, was the Oklahoma Military Institute, incorporated in 1903 as a prep school for young men from Indian and Oklahoma Territories. The academy closed shortly thereafter and reopened as the Oklahoma College for Young Ladies. The structure burned in 1909.

The year 1904 also brought the first flour mill in Oklahoma City, established by George G. Solbert, who was president of the Acme Milling Company.

The Sydney L. Brock Dry Goods Company was organized in 1906 at 213 West Main Street, with a twenty-five-foot storefront. It operated as the Brock Store until 1915 when it was sold to Rorabaugh-Brown, and developed into the John A. Brown Store, covering nearly a full block, and with several branch stores.

By 1906 building permits totaled $2.5 million and the number was doubled the next year. A half-mile of brick business blocks were built in Oklahoma City that year. Most were of modern construction, and many were fireproof. The most elaborate was the new office building for

*The second Santa Fe Depot was under construction in 1904 when this picture was taken. It was torn down in 1930 and replaced by the present depot structure.*

the Pioneer Telephone Company on the northwest corner of Northwest Third and Broadway, completed in 1907 at a cost of about $200,000. This building is today the oldest building in downtown Oklahoma City in its original exterior style.

In September 1907 the Oklahoma Railway Company contracted with the Belle Isle Improvement Company to use Belle Isle Park's water supply to generate power and to use park land for a power plant. The power plant was completed in 1910. The park was developed for fishing, swimming, thrill rides, and a variety of entertainment.

*An aerial view illustration of Delmar Garden, a 140-acre amusement park, from a 1905 postcard.*

Between the years of Delmar Garden and Springlake, Belle Isle was the principal amusement and entertainment park in the city. It was also in 1907 that the Maywood Presbyterian Church was built on the southeast corner of Ninth and Stiles of Romanesque style, in the Maywood district. This building, which served the Maywood congregation until 1985, was remodeled for headquarters for the HTB Architects and now serves as headquarters for the Oklahoma Department of Commerce.

Market day at Statehood time was Saturday mornings, with farmers and merchants bringing their products on weekends to the 100 block of West California Street.

The Daughters of the American Revolution organized in the city in 1904, and a chapter of the United Daughters of the Confederacy started the next year. Other women's clubs at the time were Philomathea, The Bible, Twentieth Century, New Century, Cosmopolitan, Renaissance, Cosmos, and Sans Souci. Among the men's organizations were the Masons, Odd Fellows, Knights of Pythias, Knights of Columbus, Woodsmen of the World, Modern Woodsmen, Elks, and Eagles.

The Oklahoma State Fair, replacing the Territorial Fair, was organized and opened its gates in 1907, barely over one month before statehood. It was located a mile east of the city where alfalfa had been grown and harvested barely a year earlier. It had exhibition halls, cement walls, a grandstand with a race track, and many other accessories. People were brought to the fair by shuttle, furnished by the KATY Railroad, because the streetcar lines had not yet been extended to that location. The fair opened October 5, 1907, and closed on October 16. Total attendance was seventy-five thousand people.

That year W. T. Hales started his horse and mule market in Oklahoma City. He earned much of his fortune selling mules during World War 1. As a result, he

The Oklahoma City Chamber of Commerce Band of 1906 participated in numerous local events, in addition to making the annual Oklahoma City Goodwill Tour to various Oklahoma communities.

A large crowd of people from Oklahoma County and adjacent counties jostle each other to greet the arrival of New York Governor Theodore Roosevelt for the Rough Riders Reunion in 1900.

became one of the principal property owners downtown.

Statehood on November 16, 1907, brought many things to Oklahoma, one of which was Prohibition, which Federal legislation in the Enabling Act had required of the Constitution. On that day 46 saloons in Oklahoma City and 500 others in the state closed their doors at 11:50 p.m.

At the time of statehood, *Peck's Bad Boy* was playing at the Overholser Opera House. *Happy Hooligan* was featured in the comic strips. The Keeley Institute at Northwest Twenty-fifth and University Boulevard was advertising a cure for whiskey drinking and drug and tobacco addictions. Oklahoma City's population at statehood was fourteen thousand.

Motion pictures of the silent variety were growing in popularity. One popular

theater which opened at 320 West Grand in 1909 was the Metropolitan. There Lon Chaney worked as a stagehand after working at the Overholser Opera House.

The year of statehood was also the year of organization of the city's first country club—Lakeview Country Club in the Maywood addition in east Oklahoma City. This became the Oklahoma City Golf and Country Club in 1912, moving later to Northwest Thirty-ninth and Western (site of the present Crown Heights Christian Church), and later to Nichols Hills. A choice eating spot in 1907 was the American Lunch Room at 19 South Broadway, which boasted linen tablecloths, napkins, electric fans and palm plants.

The Western Newspaper Union announced that year that it was building an imposing six-story fireproof structure

at the southwest corner of Second and Harvey. A Federal Building site was located at Northwest Third Street between Robinson and Harvey.

The street railway system had enlarged greatly. It had gone near bankruptcy in 1904 and Anton Classen purchased the interests of W. W. Storm, enlarged the lines, and changed the name of the company from Metropolitan Railway Company to the Oklahoma City Railway Company. More than four million persons were transported in 1907, with about 38 miles of track, 48 cars, and 150 employees. A new water plant was being completed, costing $255,000, paid through a bond issue. The city had nine financial institutions, including five national banks, three state banks and one trust company. Oklahoma County had a population of more than 50,000, with 32,451 in Oklahoma City. Oklahoma County had an area of 720 square miles. Real and personal property value in the county was $8.25 million.

At year's end in 1908, brickwork was complete on the seven story Majestic building, work was started on increasing the Security Building from three to six stories, and it was announced that the Campbell Building would be raised from four to nine stories.

A tragedy occurred in 1908 when the Lee Hotel burned to the ground in a fire which could be seen as far away as Edmond to the north and Harrah to the east. The adjacent Campbell Building was partially damaged. The hotel was rebuilt following the fire to become the Lee-Huckins, and later the Huckins.

The Lion Store, at Main and Robinson, which was destroyed earlier by fire, was replaced by the Lee Office Building, which in later years housed the American, Fidelity, and Liberty National Banks. More recently it became the Oil and Gas Building and was wrapped in metal. Still later the metal was removed, it was re-bricked, and joins the Pioneer building as one of the two oldest buildings in downtown Oklahoma City.

*Looking north from Grand at a parade on Broadway, c. 1910.*

# CHAPTER IV

## OKLAHOMA CITY, CAPITAL OF OKLAHOMA

As it entered a new decade, Oklahoma City had a population of 50,000 and 70 miles of asphalt streets, scores of large office buildings, and fine schools, churches and residences. During its first twenty years, the city had obtained many industries which served cities and towns statewide as well as surrounding states, but up to this time had no industry serving nationwide consumers.

Being in the center of a livestock region, business leaders had worked toward developing a major livestock industry. Opportunity came in 1910 when Morris and Company of Chicago began looking at the Oklahoma City market. Largely through the efforts of Sidney Brock, who operated the Brock Store, money was raised to secure this plant. The Oklahoma City facility of Morris and Company gave birth to packing town in the Capitol Hill area. This organization later became Armour and Company. A second major meat packing company came soon afterwards, which later became Wilson and Company.

The year 1910 was a major construction period for Oklahoma City—possibly the biggest in its history, considering the size of the city at that time. One structure which was completed during that year was the Colcord Building at Grand and Robinson, which, because of its twelve stories, was dubbed Oklahoma City's first skyscraper. Also completed were the Baum Building, across the street from the Colcord; the State National Bank, which later became the Hales Building; and Central High School, farther north on Robinson. Under construction was the Skirvin Hotel, completed the following year. Also under construction, in packingtown, was the Livestock Exchange Building, providing office space for the seventeen commission firms operating at the yards. On Broadway, across from the Huckins, an office building was under construction for Bass and Harbour, which would house Oklahoma Gas &Electric Company for a number of years, and which later would be known as the Insurance Building..

On Main Street S. H. Kress and Company, which had opened in a small three story building, expanded to incorporate a building to its east, and Frederickson-Kroh Music Company opened a wholesale and retail music store on Main Street.

But something else, even bigger was coming. Ever since the days of the Run of 1889, there had been a dispute among towns in the territory as to where the state capital would be located. More than once, elections for a state capital were held (or attempted). Sometimes through technicalities and partisan politics, Guthrie was able to retain it. When the enabling act, creating the Constitutional Convention was written by Congress, it stated that under Statehood, the capital would remain in Guthrie for the first six years, which would make 1913 the first year the capital could be removed. On June 11, 1910, an election was held for state capital location between Oklahoma City, Guthrie and Shawnee. Most people assumed that if Oklahoma City or Shawnee won, the move would be in 1913. Governor Haskell,

*The Oklahoma Railway Company powerhouse of 1910, which later became a secondary power plant of OG&E. It was removed in the early 1960s.*

who had been at odds with Guthrie and some of the city leaders since the Constitutional Convention days, went to his home in Muskogee to vote. However, when he learned that Oklahoma City was leading both of the other contenders, he called his secretary, W. B. Anthony, telling him to remove items from his Guthrie office and take them to Oklahoma City, because he was opening the next day in the Huckins Hotel. Oklahoma City was not ready to accommodate the state offices, and Guthrie, of course, was livid. This is what began the myth that the moving of the state seal was the cause of the removal of the capital. Guthrie took the case to court, and eventually to the Supreme Court of the United States, which ruled that the federal government could not tell a state where its capital would be after it became a state. This nullified that portion of the Enabling Act.

Initially Oklahoma City housed the various state departments in business buildings downtown. The Legislature held its meetings in the ballroom of the Shrine building on the northwest corner of Second and Broadway (a structure now incorporated

into the Kerr-McGee complex). It would not be until the time of World War I, that a State Capitol building would be constructed.

Governor Haskell was destined to serve his final year and a half as governor in his Huckins Hotel office in Oklahoma City before a new governor—Lee Cruce of Ardmore—would succeed him.

One of the first actions of the Cruce administration was the creation of what would become one of the most important departments in the State of Oklahoma. Automobiles had begun to appear on Oklahoma streets and on the country roads. An improved road was considered to be one covered with gravel. By the turn of the second decade, automobiles were fast replacing the horse and wagon as a means of transportation. This resulted in the Oklahoma Legislature creating the State Highway Department, now known as the Oklahoma Department of Transportation, in March 1911. In the same month the office of state fire marshal of Oklahoma was created.

In the cultural area, the Art League of Oklahoma City was formed in 1911,

following a local art exhibit. Charles F. Colcord was elected its first president. It began with 150 members, but during its first season the membership more than doubled. Over the years it grew into the Allied Arts Foundation of Oklahoma City, which remains active and influential in the cultural life of Oklahoma City, encompassing both visual and performing arts.

Sports in general, including auto racing and boxing, had become popular in Oklahoma City in this pre-World War I period. The leading auto racers of the time were among those performing in Oklahoma City on a course on Linwood. In 1915 the immortal Barney Oldfield put on a race which drew fourteen thousand spectators. Jess Willard, who became a world champion boxer, got his start in Oklahoma City, migrated to the East and West Coasts, later winning the world's heavyweight championship by knocking out Jack Johnson in Havana.

The State Fair of Oklahoma was growing. Total attendance at the sixth annual State Fair was 130,000 and the number of exhibitors totaled 1,459. By the turn of the twenty-first century paid attendance has risen to one and one-half million.

Early 1913 brought the worst snowstorm in the history of Oklahoma. On February 3, Oklahoma City recorded seven inches of snow. A year and a half later, shortages of water brought about a proclamation that citizens of Oklahoma City could use water only two hours daily. No main reservoir had yet been constructed in the city, and Lake Overholser was another four years away. The migration of manufacturing companies to Oklahoma had reduced considerably because of a shortage of water.

Henry Ford came to Oklahoma City in 1915 to establish a Model T assembly plant on West Main Street, east of Classen. Within a year the plant was turning out 244 autos a day. One employee in the plant was a man by the name of Fred Jones, who, by 1922, had his own automobile agency in Oklahoma City and later purchased the plant as a rebuilding facility.

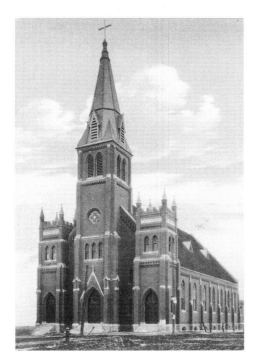

*St. Joseph's Catholic Church at Northwest Fourth and Harvey is one of only two churches in Oklahoma City on property occupied by the church in 1889. It was badly damaged by the 1995 bombing of the Murrah Building, but was restored and enlarged.*

War was underway in Europe, but it did not stop Oklahoma from starting construction on its long-planned State Capitol Building. Since obtaining the capital in mid-1910, plans had been underway for the building, and several developers and organizations were competing for the site. One was South Oklahoma City, which proposed a location, and gave birth to its identification as Capitol Hill (spelled with an o instead of an a). Other competitors were I. M. Putnam, who was developing Putnam Heights and other residential areas, and John Shartel, who was the principal in the Oklahoma City-El Reno interurban line. The land Putnam offered was west of Oklahoma City, where he offered 1,600 acres of land and $1.7 million in cash to the state for the location of its capitol. Later much of the land was given for school use, which resulted in the Putnam City school district. The site finally chosen for the Capitol was south of Northeast Twenty-third Street on land given by two adjacent developers—William F. Harn and J. J. Culbertson. Construction began on July 25, 1914. Concurrent with the beginning of construction, the executive mansion site was selected east of the future Capitol building. However, the building of the mansion was more than a dozen years away.

The Capitol, dedicated in 1917, was built for a cost of less than twenty-five cents per cubic foot—a figure far below the cost of most state capitols. The "saucer dome," with its great expanse of glass, was expected to give more natural light in the building than any other capitol in the nation. However, the building had been designed by its architect, Solomon Layton, to include a dome, and the question of adding a dome has been argued over the years. At the turn of the twenty-first century, the addition of the dome has become one of the principal goals of the state's centennial celebration, and its completion was nearing at this publication's press time.

A youth organization, begun in England and established in the United States in 1910, came officially to Oklahoma City in 1914. What became the Last Frontier Boy Scout Council was organized, with J. C. Masters, principal of Central High School, as the first president. Allen Street, later to become mayor of Oklahoma City, was Scoutmaster of one of the dozen troops initially formed in the county. Early camping was at Camp Trosper—now Trosper Park.

In 1915 the Oklahoma City Public Market opened for business on Exchange Avenue, once the site of Delmar Garden. This quickly became a popular spot for people of Oklahoma County seeking fresh vegetables and lower prices. After all, food prices were rising, partially as a result of World War I. For an example, earlier in the year the price of a loaf of bread rose from 5 to 6 cents.

By this time the city and county were becoming more modernistic. On July 15 the county assessor's office reported that for the first time automobiles outnumbered the horses in Oklahoma City—1,900 to 1,353. The automobile business was growing fast. The first Dodge dealer in the county was the McClelland-Gentry firm. The Chrisman Company was the first Buick agency. Sandy Brooks handled the Franklin, which was the pioneer air-cooled car. Ray Stapleton had the REO agency. M. H. Randall had the Chevrolet agency. Another early day dealer was Baird Markham, who later moved to New York to become director of the national association in the Petroleum Industry. A building which still bears the imprint of his name is immediately north of the YMCA Building (formerly the Oklahoman building) at Northwest Fourth and Broadway.

By the following year—1916—during the dry period of the year, a chronic water problem was so acute that only a two day supply was on hand. Preparations were underway for drilling a test well in the area, expected to produce two million gallons of water a day to help alleviate the water shortage. The water problem was twofold because during parts of the year there was flooding on the North Canadian River. However, city fathers had become serious about solving the problem. On May 20 a civic improvement bond issue election provided one and one-half million dollars

*A near-downtown scene in Oklahoma City about the time of World War I.*

The First Christian Church at Northwest Tenth and Robinson was built in 1910. The church is now located in a domed structure at Northwest Thirty-sixth and Walker, on property which was the location of the Edgemere Golf and Country Club.

for construction of a dam and creation of a storage basin capable of holding 6.8 million gallons of water. This was destined to become Lake Overholser, named for Ed Overholser, then mayor of Oklahoma City and son of the pioneer developer, Henry Overholser.

Active in the civic community was the Oklahoma City Chamber of Commerce, which in 1916 obtained quarters on Main Street. That year also brought about the creation of the Tenth Circuit Court of Appeals, composed of Oklahoma, Arkansas, Tennessee and the northern district of Alabama and Mississippi. Also organized during the year was the Lakeside Country Club, which grew to 250 members in its first five years. It was planned to construct a $10,000 building near the planned city lake and lay out an eighteen-hole golf course.

However, there were international threats, both to the east and to the south. War was raging in Europe. Although President Wilson won his second term on the slogan, "He kept us out of war," it seemed inevitable that America would become involved. The other threat was to the south, where Pancho Villa was waving swords from Mexico. In June 1916 National Guard units, including the Oklahoma National Guard, were ordered to federal service on the Mexican border. This turned out to be caution duty only, without military action. Meanwhile, fighting in Europe became more heated, and the sinking of the American vessel *Lusitania* brought the United States into the war.

The Oklahoma National Guard had been dismissed from active duty barely a month before it was called again—this time for combat in World War I. The Guard, then called the First Oklahoma Infantry, did not fight as a single unit. Most of its members were assigned to the Ninetieth Infantry Division, best known as the T-O Division (Texas and Oklahoma). Others went to the Seventy-eighth (Rainbow) Division. Most of them saw combat in the battle of San Miguel and the Battle of the Argonne. Among troops serving in World War I, approximately 5,000 were from Oklahoma County, including 1,600 from Oklahoma City and 3,400 from other communities and farmlands in the county. One who commanded a machine gun company in the T-O Division was Raymond S. McLain, of Oklahoma City, who would later become the first National Guard officer ever to command an army corps in combat during World War II.

There was also strong support on the home front. The Housewives League, in Oklahoma County, initiated one of the first movements in the nation toward self-denial to conserve food needed for the Allies in France. Books and magazines were being received by the Chamber of Commerce to be sent to Fort Sill, where there was a big demand for reading matter among the soldiers. Thanksgiving Day of 1917 brought fifteen hundred hungry solders from Fort Sill to Oklahoma County, who were taken in for dinner in homes.

By the spring of 1917 more than 10,000 home gardens had been planted in the back yards and vacant lots in Oklahoma County. An awards competition supporting the home gardening movement was sponsored by the Oklahoma Publishing Company and the Oklahoma City Chamber of Commerce.

In order to reach the young people, the superintendent of schools admonished all teachers to teach the Pledge of Allegiance, the Declaration of Independence and the Preamble to the Constitution. School children also participated in the gardening effort and a school garden contest was held.

Campaigns for Liberty Bonds were conducted. Those in the county purchased bonds of the second Liberty Loan in the amount of $3.5 million.

Despite the war, building continued in Oklahoma County. In 1917 a new $100,000 research addition was added at St. Anthony's Hospital. Other construction during the year included the Acme Milling Company, which was increasing its storage capacity up to two hundred bushels. The Oklahoma City Mill and Elevator Company added to its storage facility by building nine additional tanks with a capacity of 175,000 bushels.

The Oklahoma Furniture Manufacturing Company added a new department for manufacturing beds. The Odelsa Company came to the city to manufacture and distribute food products, including coffee, tea, spices, extracts, and baking powder. The Moco Laboratories were organized at Grand and Dewey to make the Moco Monkey Grip self-vulcanizing auto tire patches. The Oklahoma Railway Company extended its streetcar lines on Broadway from Thirteenth to Eighteenth Street, and a new line on Robinson Avenue was opened. The over-crowding of schools brought about a successful bond issue providing enlargements for six schools and a new elementary school (Wilson School) at Northwest Twentieth and Walker.

In the fall of 1918 Oklahoma City was the victim of Spanish Influenza which was sweeping the country. Several deaths occurred in Oklahoma County before the disease was identified and its seriousness appreciated. Within a few days the president of the Oklahoma County Medical Association announced that there were more than a thousand cases in Oklahoma County. All public schools, theaters and churches were closed. The death toll in Oklahoma City was about three hundred.

The year 1919 was described as a year of prosperity and high prices. Money was plentiful and the spending of it was very free. There were high food prices, high clothes

*Morris and Company, later Armour, packing plant, c. 1910.*

*This artist's rendering of the Colcord Building at Robinson and Grand shows the building with two wings, but the second wing was never constructed. Opened in 1910, the building was once touted as "Oklahoma City's first skyscraper."*

prices and high rental costs. It was described by some as "an era of silk shirts, two bit cigars, $3,000 motor cars, short skirts, and the immodest exhibition of female limbs." Investigation of wholesale and retail prices was demanded. Oklahoma County Attorney Robert Burns was petitioned by more than one hundred residents to call a grand jury. Judge C. B. Ames, then assistant to the Attorney General of the United States, opened the investigation of the high cost of living and charges of profiteering.

Shoes had gone from seven dollars to twenty dollars, plus the war tax. Beef, at wholesale, went from ten cents to eighteen cents a pound. Sugar reached the high point of twenty-one cents a pound. Hotel rooms which once rented for one dollar were now bringing five dollars. Residence rentals which were bringing $25 a month were now bringing $65. Salaries were up, but not proportionally.

In June, Oklahoma County was decked out to welcome her sons of the Thirty-sixth Division. A parade downtown was headed by a float of flower girls.

During the year an eight hour day for Oklahoma County employees was adopted by the county commissioners.

There was considerable interest in whether there would be enough jobs in Oklahoma County for the returning

soldiers. However, a questionnaire to businesses brought response indicating that there were plenty of jobs available. Of 596 soldiers who came back and asked for their old jobs, 560 got them. Of the remainder, thirty-one declined to go to work at the prevailing wages, and only eight employers were unable to employ all the men who had left the jobs.

In October 1919 the American Legion was created in Oklahoma and the first meeting was held in Oklahoma City for the State of Oklahoma.

A million dollar school bond campaign for more and better schools in Oklahoma City was a big success with the issue carrying by almost six to one. The money provided three new junior high schools, including the land, along with extensive improvements for 11 of the city's 28 elementary schools.

Construction began on a new $100,000 Liberal Arts building at the State Fairgrounds, to be completed one month before the opening of the 1919 State Fair.

After a careful survey of the situation, it was shown that there was a serious shortage of homes in Oklahoma City, which greatly hampered industrial development. An advertising campaign was started to urge prospective builders to "build your home first."

This late 1920s view of Oklahoma City looking northwest over the Santa Fe railroad tracks shows the Biltmore Hotel.

# CHAPTER V

A DECADE OF PROSPERITY

The 1920s brought to Oklahoma and to Oklahoma County a decade of prosperity and growth. The 1920 census count showed the population of Oklahoma City to be 91,258, an increase of 42 percent over the 54,168 persons enumerated in 1910. The decade was also the beginning of what might today be called the women's liberation movement. The Nineteenth Amendment gave women the right to vote. Oklahoma had an estimated 392,000 women eligible to vote in the November election of 1920. An Oklahoma woman—Alice Robertson of Muskogee—was the first woman to be elected to congress. However, a woman who had migrated to Oklahoma City set a more impressive record thirteen years earlier, before women had received the right to vote, when Kate Barnard was the first of her sex in the nation to be elected to a state office. She was Oklahoma's commissioner of charities and corrections, elected at the beginning of statehood in 1907, and served two four-year terms.

However, the women's movement of the 1920s was not limited to the right to vote. It was the decade of the "flapper." The right to smoke was another of the demands. The cigarette companies were catering to this prospective new market with such ads as "You've come a long way, baby," and the motion pictures were featuring the most glamorous stars sporting cigarettes. This was not without protest from the men. On February 21, 1920, there was a demonstration of protest against the establishment of a smoking room for women at an automobile show which was scheduled to be held in Oklahoma City the following month.

Discovery of oil in eastern and, later, southern Oklahoma had brought some investments in Oklahoma City, but it was not until after the Cushing Field discovery that large numbers of investors began to bring to Oklahoma City the fruits of their explorations. The Cushing pool developed a daily production of three hundred thousand barrels of crude oil. Discovery of oil at Healdton may be credited for the

spirit of adventure known as wildcatting. Many Oklahoma City people made their first oil investments there. During the next six years, Oklahoma City acquired its reputation as an oil center. By 1921 it was known that Oklahoma City was near the geographic center of the oil producing area of the state. Oklahoma City became a promotion center and attracted business prospects from all of the country, as well as foreign countries. Oil was more responsible than any other natural resource. Oklahoma City became the home of more men engaged in the oil business than any other city of the Southwest. It also became one of the principal refining centers. At the beginning of 1921 more than one hundred oil companies had offices in Oklahoma City. Most of them had producing properties in Oklahoma.

Besides being the main headquarters for many oil interests, it was a major operating office of the Santa Fe Railroad and the home office of the Shaffer Refining Company, which later, in 1921, was sold to the H. M. Byllesby Company of Chicago, which also owned the Oklahoma Gas and Electric Company.

In 1919 Oklahoma City had become an administrative headquarters for the Magnolia Petroleum Company for Oklahoma and Kansas and built the office building which still stands on North Broadway. The Josey Oil Company moved its general office to Oklahoma City from Yale. It was the area headquarters for the Atlantic Oil Producing Company and for the National Oil and Development Company. The Texas Company established the sales department of its refining division in Oklahoma City. The city was a distribution center for the Marland Refining Company of Ponca City, which later became Conoco. The Empire Gas and Fuel Company operated the first crude oil refinery in Oklahoma City.

Also experiencing growth were the milling and grain business, which had increased one hundred percent in Oklahoma City during the ten years prior to 1921. This industry employed two thousand people and had a payroll of $2 million a year. Five mills were operating in 1921, and five feed companies were also operating. Flour mills were operated by the Oklahoma City Mill and Elevator Company, Acme Milling, the Plan Sifter Milling Company, the Belt Mill and Grain Company and the Stockyards Milling Company. It also had a branch of the Yukon Mill and Grain Company. There was a six-story grain exchange building and most of the grain dealers had offices there. In 1920 Oklahoma produced about forty-five thousand bushels of wheat, virtually all handled by Oklahoma City millers.

The beginning of the decade also marked the announcement of plans for a new street car terminal, to be located on Grand Avenue between Harvey and Hudson, at a cost of $200,000. A block to its east, also on Grand Avenue, construction began that year on the twelve-story Oklahoma Club, which, for most of the next three decades, would be the premier downtown social and luncheon club in Oklahoma City.

Farther from town, northwest of Oklahoma City, and near the El Reno

*Bathing beauties in Northeast Park (now Lincoln Park) Lake in 1920.*

interurban car line, a camp for children was established by the Lions Clubs in June 1920. It was called Camp Lybrand, in honor of Walter Lybrand, a club member who was among the most active. Later the club moved to a site in Edmond—later the Lions Fun Park.

Politics loomed large in Oklahoma City in the early 1920s. The powerful postwar political figure was John Walton, mayor of the city. Opponents of his administration, including both newspapers, carried on a bitter campaign against the two commissioners who were running to succeed themselves. These opponents made the issue anti-Walton, rather than an attack on the records of each other. The mayor was accused of extravagance and of undue bent toward labor unions. They also charged the mayor and city government of supporting organization of a union among policemen and with the distribution of thousands of courtesy cards, known as special police commissions. As a result, the Republican nominees opposing the administration were elected by over twenty-five hundred votes. During the first meeting after the election, the board took the police department away from the

mayor and declared the courtesy cards no longer valid.

In April 1921 complaints were made to the Health Department that the ordinance requiring ownership of cows in the city to one per residence was being violated.

The year 1921 was also a year of excessive rains. In June, after heavy rains, the levees in south Oklahoma City were reinforced with a crest of twelve feet. The next month a rainfall measuring 2.3 inches fell in Oklahoma City in a period of two hours.

The theory behind radio had been discovered by Guglielmo Marconi earlier in the century, but its commercial use was slow in starting. Before World War I, there were a few stations in the east, but none west of the Mississippi River, and few beyond the east coast. This was to end as the third decade began. Opening in a small wooden building, Oklahoma City's WKY became the first radio station west of the Mississippi River. This became a major means of entertainment, as people listened to music, news, and commentary, all produced locally.

In 1922 the Oklahoma County Tuberculosis Hospital opened in a building

*The interior of a grocery store at 1014 West Fourth Street in 1922.*

earlier used by the girls industrial home northeast of Oklahoma City.

The same year brought about the opening of the first long stretch of hard surface highway in Oklahoma County, which extended ten miles of test paving, which ran east and west, north of the State Capitol—now Northeast Twenty-third Street. Other paving was planned, or was underway. In fact, by the end of 1922, nearly 150 miles of streets were paved with asphalt, brick or concrete. A concrete road was under construction on Northwest Avenue (now called Western) to the town of Britton. To serve travelers in the area between Oklahoma City and Britton (then an incorporated town), a tourist court was planned, to be constructed east of Belle Isle Park.

Post-war construction was underway. The Braniff Insurance Company constructed a ten-story building in 1923 at Northwest Third and Robinson. Tom Braniff was then well-known in Oklahoma City, but later, when he formed Braniff Airlines, he became internationally famous.

Bids were opened that year for the new Federal Reserve Bank Building to be constructed at Northwest Third and Harvey. The Rotary Club was asking for bids for the purchase of about $110,000

in equipment for the children's playground in Rotary Park. The University Hospital on Northeast Thirteenth Street was being enlarged, and an addition was being made to the Mount St. Mary's Academy in south Oklahoma City.

However, that period also brought unemployment. Contributions were asked by the United Provident Association to furnish unemployed people with beds at 127 West Grand. Cots were installed and were occupied every night. The Oklahoma City Chamber of Commerce was enlarging its employment service, working with other civic groups. OG&E announced that it would supply current for electric fans free of charge for indigent sick individuals throughout the summer.

Advertisements in newspapers in this period told of companies which existed during that post-World War I period, and a few still exist today, including the Macklanburg-Duncan Company, Standard Engraving Company, and OG&E. Other well-remembered companies were the Big Four Ice and Delivery Company, Leonard and Braniff Mortgage and Loan Company, First National Bank, Oklahoma City Mill and Elevator Company, New State Ice Cream Company, G.A. Nichols Real Estate, Mideke Supply Company, Oklahoma Sash and Door Company, Oklahoma

Multigraphing Company, Western Newspaper Union, the Rorabaugh-Brown Company, and Oklahoma Carriage and Auto Works.

The growth of Oklahoma City brought about the beginning of community agencies, which have grown over the years and have played increasingly important roles in the development of the city. One was its first Community Chest, with Judge C. B. Ames as chairman of the organizing committee. Another was the Oklahoma City Better Business Bureau, with more than $700 subscribed for its establishment.

Higher education also took a big step forward that year. It had been more than twelve years since the closing of Epworth University, and the nearest institutions of higher learning were Central State Normal (now the University of Central Oklahoma) in Edmond, and the University of Oklahoma in Norman. But in this boom period, the Methodists were building a new facility at Northwest Twenty-third and Blackwelder—Oklahoma City College, which later became Oklahoma City University.

Oklahoma City continued to be a center for entertainment. The Overholser Opera House downtown had been sold to the Sinopoulos, who had earlier developed Delmar Garden. It became an Orpheum Theater, bringing in the entertainment of the Orpheum circuit. A building nearby, was known as the City Auditorium, although it was not owned or operated by the city. The completion of the Shrine Theater, in what later was the Journal Record Building, was still two years away. However, a popular auditorium for public events was in Central High School. It brought many well known performers, such as Madame Schumenn-Heink, who gave a concert performance there in 1922. Another popular, and fairly new entertainment spot was the Coliseum, in the Stockyards area.

Providing building sites for residential purposes was a problem brought about by a population surge. No residential development had been opened since before the beginning of World War I, but in 1922 G. A. Nichols, a dentist turned developer, began building on the old Epworth tract and in the Gatewood area.

It was in 1921 that he acquired the forty-acre tract west of Classen between Northwest Seventeenth and Twenty-first Streets, where he and other builders constructed seventy-five upper medium and high priced homes. The value of these homes ranged from $5,000 to $25,000. The following year he began developing the Gatewood addition.

Ways and means of obtaining a permanent aviation field for Oklahoma City were under consideration. For more than two years a field had been operated south of the city along the Norman interurban line. The lease of the field, however, was due to expire in 1922. One problem was devising a way to purchase the property from someone who would permit it to be used for aviation. At the same time, the matter of organizing a permanent National Guard Air Squadron was underway.

By the beginning of 1923 there were 35 commercial printing establishments, operating 30 flatbed presses and 123 job presses with a daily total of 1.5 million printed impressions.

The same year saw the opening of a new outdoor market across from the YMCA on Second Street, near the area now occupied by Kerr Park. The original market was located at Grand and Harvey, and was such a success that its developers considered a second market to be justified only a few blocks away.

Wild animals became pests, and sometimes a hazard, in parts of Oklahoma County. To help alleviate this situation, a wolf hunt was held west of the town of Britton. This was the second such effort in the vicinity.

Politics was rampant in 1922. John Walton, who had experienced a stormy career as mayor of Oklahoma City, ran for governor of Oklahoma and won. His inauguration party—an outdoor barbecue—brought to Oklahoma City the largest number of visitors the city had ever experienced. However, his popularity

statewide was not long lived. In April 1923 he commissioned sixty secret service agents to enforce prohibition laws throughout the state whenever local officers failed to do so. He often used the National Guard to enforce law or to quell problems. In June 1923 he declared martial law for Okmulgee County, sending troops to Henryetta and Okmulgee because of what Walton called "mob rule." Soon efforts were underway for his impeachment, and he called out the National Guard to prevent the legislature from convening for the impeachment effort. However, it didn't work, and Walton was the first of two successively elected

*Ladies storm the state capitol in 1923 when Governor Walton refused to allow the legislature, which was planning his impeachment, to meet.*

governors to be removed from office by the legislature.

Business in Oklahoma City was prospering. It was reported that ninety-five percent of Oklahoma's automobiles were being sold from Oklahoma City. A newspaper story pointed out that in a six-month period there was hauled to the Oklahoma National Stockyards 31,319 cattle, 67,010 hogs, and 5,782 sheep.

Construction was rampant. The Terminal Building for the electric streetcar system was underway for Grand Avenue west of Harvey. The Physicians Building, later called the Medical Arts Building, was getting underway at Broadway and First Street (now Park Avenue). Construction was starting on the new Shrine Building (later Home State Life and, still later, the

Journal Record Building). Plans were underway for adding a new wing east on the Skirvin Hotel, doubling its size. A campaign was underway to raise $400,000 to enlarge the state Baptist Hospital at Northwest Twelfth and Walker from a 35-bed institution to one with 200 beds. Its name was to be changed to Oklahoma City General Hospital. Later it became Mercy Hospital. A Trader's Cotton Compress was completed just outside Oklahoma City's corporate limits at Reno and Eastern, and boasted being the largest compress west of the Mississippi River. The year also marked the installation of

the first dial telephones in Oklahoma, installed by Southwestern Bell.

The Oklahoma Gas and Electric Company, founded in 1902 and headquartered in Oklahoma City, had expanded statewide and into Western Arkansas by this time. During its earlier period, it had been acquiring small companies and municipal electric systems, using their small local generating stations to produce the electricity to serve the system. Oklahoma City's electric needs were served principally by generators in its operating headquarters at Broadway and Noble Streets (later Southwest Third Street). It was in 1923 that the company built its first large generator, designed for high voltage distribution throughout its

*The boathouse at Belle Isle Park in the early 1920s.*

service area. This was the Horseshoe Lake Generating Station, which the company opened in Harrah in eastern Oklahoma County. Besides marking the beginning of system-wide transmission for the company, the Horseshoe Lake Station was a boon for Harrah, providing a large number of skilled jobs in the town.

Parks and schools were also benefiting from this building boom. Northeast Park (later Lincoln Park) sported a bathing beach. Wheeler Park, near the North Canadian River, was the home of the Oklahoma City Zoo, although its days were numbered. Belle Isle Park, owned by the Oklahoma Street Railway Company and adjacent to the city on the north side, had a bathing beach, rowboats and the usual Coney Island attractions which thrilled young and old alike. More than five thousand people visited the park each day, according to reports of 1923. Efforts were underway to develop a park project on land bounded by Eleventh, Fourteenth, McKinley, and Douglas Streets in the western part of the city, with the community's finest playgrounds. This became McKinley Park.

A building program was also underway for the Oklahoma City Public Schools. Contracts were let for an addition of 4 to 12 rooms in several

schools. A new building was constructed on the grounds of the Lee Elementary School, relieving the necessity for half-day sessions. Substantial additions were made to three junior high schools and the completion of the Roosevelt and Harding Junior High Schools. Classen was converted into a senior high school, and with the Central and Irving buildings, there was enough space for all high school students. The Horace Mann and Spivey Schools were built to care for children in a new area for which

they served. This left Oklahoma City with only Harmony, Gatewood, Mulligan, Rockwood, and Longfellow not provided with brick buildings. Temporary plans provided portable structures for those schools.

Although Oklahoma's capital city was known as Oklahoma City since the time of the Run, it was called Oklahoma, Oklahoma, by the federal post office, and it was not until 1923, and then at the insistence of the Chamber of Commerce, that the government agreed to accept the change of name.

Oklahoma City Beautiful and Edmond Beautiful are well known organizations at the turn of the twenty-first century, but although the organizations were formed in the last thirty-five years, the term originated in the first quarter of the last century. It originated in 1923 when the Town Club, one of the most influential of the women's civic clubs, using the theme, "Oklahoma City Beautiful," conducted an intensive clean-up week and sponsored many other beautification activities. During that year competition was held for beautification of homes, commercial organizations, and public places. Included among first-place winners were the Marland service station at Northwest Seventeenth and Classen, the Morris packing plant, which was beautifully

*Flooding on what was then known as Choctaw Street, near the North Canadian River south of downtown Oklahoma City in 1923.*

Flooding near the North Canadian River on Oklahoma City in 1923.

The rains of 1923 flooded this grocery store at the corner of California and Western.

landscaped, and the Pilgrim Congregational Church. A tree-planting effort was also underway as a result of the Oklahoma Nurserymen's Association and the Oklahoma Florist Association.

The downside of 1923, however, was the flood. Heavy rains in the spring forced the opening of floodgates to prevent the Overholser Dam from breaking. All of downtown Oklahoma City was flooded. Wheeler Park, just north of the river, was the worst hit, and the animals in the zoo had to be removed immediately. The move was to a new permanent location in Northeast Park, later re-named Lincoln Park. In its new location the Zoo later gained national reputation as one of the ten finest zoos in the nation.

As for the flood, five alligators were found in Oklahoma City, and one theory was that they had come from the swollen Red River.

The following year marked the formal opening of the new Municipal Aviation Field of Oklahoma, celebrated by the largest air circus ever held, to that time, in the area. The field, south of Oklahoma City, was leased by the Chamber of Commerce, and was used as a municipal airport. The celebration was participated in by planes from five different Army posts as well as commercial planes from throughout the Southwest.

Two buildings were going up on North Harvey in 1924, barely over a block apart. On the southeast corner of Northwest Second and Harvey, the six-story, fireproof Cotton Exchange building was opened. Its tenants included dealers and specialists in Oklahoma's greatest farm products, particularly cotton. This structure later became the Leonhardt Building, and now is known as Court Plaza. The other structure was the half million dollar new home of the Elks Lodge at Northwest Third and Harvey, recognized as one of the finest Elks Lodges in the Southwest. This building later became the Key Building, and currently is the Oklahoma City headquarters for Oklahoma Natural Gas Company. Farther south, on West Main Street, a new eight-story building was under construction for the Kerr Dry Goods Company.

The next two years brought new growth and challenges. Through the support of the Chamber, Oklahoma City averted the threat of losing its two meat packing plants in 1925. The next year brought the beginning of air mail to Oklahoma City, with 314 pounds of airmail being mailed out of Oklahoma City the first day. The first airmail plane was named Miss Oklahoma City. There was a minimum traffic requirement of thirteen hundred average letters to make up this guarantee. The postage rate was ten cents an ounce, or a fraction thereof, for a city to remain on the air mail routes. When it appeared that Oklahoma City was not going to meet this requirement in the early years, the Chamber mailed dummy air mail letters to various destinations to make up the difference.

The year also brought a new Oklahoma City radio station, KFJF, which boasted "the most modern equipment and the best talent available." The station preceded its announcements with, "Oklahoma City— The City of Opportunity."

Industry and commerce continued to build. Eighty new industries and companies came into Oklahoma City during the first six months of 1926. In addition, more than two hundred new families established homes in the city. One was the American Iron and Machine Works, which secured a location on the Rock Island tracks.

Under construction was the Petroleum Building, Oklahoma's tallest structure, scheduled for occupancy in 1927. Also going up was the Perrine Building (later the Cravens Building and now the Robinson Renaissance Building). Away

*Horseshoe Lake Station, opened in 1923, was the first major electric power plant of OG&E serving interconnected cities and towns. For nearly eighty years it has been the largest industry in Harrah.*

*The early Central Fire Station of Oklahoma City was located east of where the Myriad was constructed.*

from downtown, construction was underway on the Mid-Continent Life Insurance Company headquarters at Classen Drive and Shartel. The Harlow Publishing Company ran an advertisement addressed to the writers of the Southwest, saying that the company is engaged in development of Southwestern authorship and the building of a southwestern publishing house.

The year 1927 brought the first under-ground electric power lines in Oklahoma City, initially constructed below Broadway. It took four years to complete the down-town underground system. OG&E also

started construction that year on its new general office building on the southwest corner of Northwest Third and Broadway. The company moved into the new building in 1928, and in the mid-1950s enlarged the structure from six to twelve stories.

Putnam Park, south of Northwest Thirty-sixth Street between Classen and Western, which had been given to the city by I. M. Putnam when the site was far out in the country, underwent major changes in 1927. The lake, which had been popular for boating, was drained, a building was added, and its name was changed to Memorial Park, honoring soldiers who lost their lives

in World War I. A fountain honoring the fallen soldiers was installed in the park.

Commercial construction continued. Wesley Hospital was expanding at Northwest Twelfth and Harvey to take care of the growing needs for Oklahoma county. Construction work was underway on Saint Anthony's hospital addition, and construction was set to begin on the University hospital, costing $300,000, at 800 East Thirteenth Street. Announcement was made by the Oklahoma City General Hospital that it would build an addition.

While bank mergers and acquisitions are common today, they are not a new development. In 1927, when First National and American National banks merged, it created the third largest bank in the Midwest. The heads of these two banks, incidentally, were brothers—Frank P. and Hugh M. Johnson.

That year brought the construction of the ten-story Commerce Exchange building on the southeast corner of Grand and Robinson. For nearly three decades, the Chamber of Commerce was in this building, occupying space on its first floor. Under construction was the Wells-Roberts Hotel, slated for opening early the next year, and the enlargement of the Skirvin Hotel, adding four stories and two hundred rooms.

However, plans were underway by Charles F. Colcord and others for a $4-million, 25-story hotel of modern Gothic Architecture. When completed two years later, it became the Biltmore Hotel, and was the central point for numerous meetings and conventions. Later this became the Sheraton Hotel, then Hotel Oklahoma, before it was demolished during urban renewal. Its location is now a part of the Myriad Gardens.

A 1927 newspaper story was published, entitled, "Local men purchase plane for business use." Since one of these men was Thomas E. Braniff, president of Braniff Investment Company, this may have been the lead-off for the organization of the Braniff Airlines. But other airlines would come first. National

Transport, Inc., which operated an airline, began service to Oklahoma City in 1927, handling airmail as well as passenger travel. Passenger fare was at the rate of ten cents per mile, making charges from Oklahoma City to Ponca City $9.20; from Oklahoma City to Wichita $16.00; to Kansas City $32.80; to Chicago $78.80; and to Dallas $21.50.

Culture was thriving in Oklahoma City. The first Oklahoma City Symphony Orchestra was in its fourth year and the city claimed the prestige of being the youngest city in the world to support a symphony. Succumbing to the depression in 1929, it would be reorganized as a WPA project in the early 1930s. The second symphony was disbanded in the late 1980s and its current successor is the Oklahoma City Philharmonic.

Art was also flourishing. Nan Sheets, an artist of note, headed the city's art gallery. The gallery was first located in the Commerce Exchange Building, then Municipal Auditorium (now Civic Center Music Hall), then to the State Fairgrounds, and finally to the remodeled former Centre Theater. A Civic Theater was organized in 1925 and its opening play, *The First Year*, was staged before a packed house at the Shrine Auditorium, which had been constructed two years earlier.

Theaters, which were converted from "silents" to "talkies," were also beginning to expand from downtown to the neighborhoods. One of the most striking was the Victoria Theater on the northwest corner of Northwest Eighteenth and Classen. This building later housed a television station that is no longer in operation, and was later converted into an office building. A second early theater away from downtown was the Capitol Hill Theater. However, construction was being started on three new theaters in Oklahoma City, with seating capacity of one thousand persons each. They were the Enenhiser, the Ritz, and the Stonewall.

Theater worker strikes in the early 1920s had resulted in combined ownership of virtually all the Oklahoma City theaters. Heading the alliance of theaters in Oklahoma City was John Sinopoulo, who had been the principal developer of Delmar Garden.

Veterans organizations were also in full swing. American Legion Post 35 was recognized as the largest Legion Post in the nation, with twenty-five hundred veteran members. A new home for Post 35 was constructed at Northwest Tenth and Robinson Streets.

An early clothing store of Oklahoma City, Barth and Myer, was a longtime leader in the clothing business in Oklahoma City when it was sold in 1927 to the Rothschild interests of Kansas and St. Louis. After the sale it was called Rothschild's B&M, and eventually the initials were dropped. The store had been founded by Sol Barth and Joe Myer in 1897.

that year to provide funds for water improvements, sanitary mains, flood control, firefighting apparatus, and traffic safety may have changed that figure.

In early 1928 Oklahoma City was reported to be the fastest growing city of its size in the United States, if the amount of building activity is a criteria. That year Oklahoma City's building total of $18 million was larger than the total building permits of any city of equal population in the country. Oklahoma City's bank deposits passed the $100 million mark in 1928, with a gain of $14 million registered for that year. It was that year that the Union Bus Station and the Union Truck Station in Oklahoma were established. New lines were extended into many areas. By the first of 1929 there were 211 towns in the Oklahoma City trade territory with overnight service.

*The Carnegie Library was constructed at Northwest Third and Robinson early in the century with funds donated by Andrew Carnegie. It was replaced by another library in the same location in the mid-1950s.*

Economically, Oklahoma City was prospering. A report from the Bureau of Government Research showed that only nine cities in the United States with a population of one hundred thousand or more had a lower per capita net bonded debt than Oklahoma City. Its outstanding debt in 1927 was $5.5 million in general improvement bonds and about the same in schools. However, a bond election later

They were served by trucks out of Oklahoma City and 110 passenger bus schedules operating in and out of the city every twenty-four hours. It was also announced in 1928 that the new auditorium of the Civic Theater Association, located at 211 West Second Street was available for meetings and conventions in Oklahoma City. The building could seat three hundred people

*The Governor's Mansion was surrounded by oil wells in the late 1920s and early 1930s.*

and had stage and dressing room facilities. A building of note, completed and dedicated in 1928, was the Governor's Mansion of Dutch Colonial Style. First to occupy the mansion was Governor Henry S. Johnston, but his stay was cut short by his impeachment.

Also coming to Oklahoma County was the first poultry colony in central Oklahoma, serving Oklahoma City's newest industry. A new suburban town, Nicoma Park, ten miles east of the State Capitol Building, sprang up as a result. Moving to Nicoma Park shortly afterwards was Oklahoma City's radio station KFJF.

Coming through Oklahoma County on Highway 66 in 1928 was a transcontinental foot race, which was popularly known as the Bunion Derby. Crossing the country from Los Angeles to New York City, the runners arrived in Oklahoma City on April 13, with the race for that day ending in front of the grandstand of the State Fairgrounds. Upon arriving in the city the racers had run 1,685 miles. The runners represented every state in the Union and several foreign countries. Although some of the contestants were among the world's most famous long distance runners, it was won by Andrew Payne from near Claremore,

an unheard of person, except in his community, who took the $25,000 first prize. Payne later served Oklahoma for many years as clerk of the Supreme Court. However, that was not the only major race coming through Oklahoma City. The other was the Transcontinental Air Race from New York to Los Angeles, which made a stop at the Oklahoma City airport, drawing a large crowd.

OG&E was in the process of purchasing Belle Isle Park from the city's electric rail transportation system, which

included an eleven-thousand-kilowatt power plant, providing electricity for the streetcar system, the interurban system and the amusement park. Upon completing the purchase in 1928, the company converted the existing generating station to serve electricity to its customers, and at the same time began construction on a new station, with three times the capacity of the existing station on Belle Isle Lake. It also built major transmission lines west to El Reno, north to Enid, and south to the company's South Broadway Station The older and smaller power plant later became a standby facility for peak loads, and was removed in the mid-1960s. The new station remained in service until the 1980s before being abandoned and sold. It was destroyed in early 1999 to make room for a new shopping center east of Penn Square.

A branch factory of the Ford Motor Company, one of Oklahoma City's largest industries, began to assemble new Ford cars at 900 West Main Street in the spring of 1928, with eight hundred men on the job. Its assembly capacity was to be 250 automobiles daily, with up to 1,500 men employed. The local plant furnished cars for all of Oklahoma, western Texas, and part of Arkansas. This plant later became the Fred Jones Manufacturing

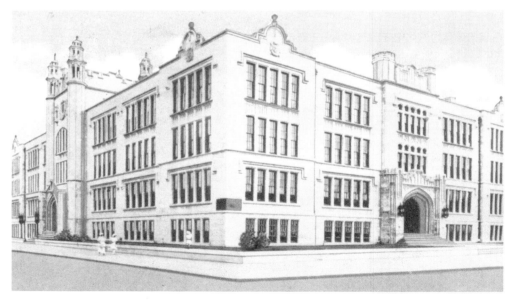

*A rendering of Central High School from a 1926 postcard.*

Looking north on Robinson from Grand from a postcard from the 1920s. The only building that remains is the Colcord Building on the far left. The building on the right is the Baum Building.

Company. That same year the Sieber Hotel, at Northwest Twelfth and Hudson was completed, and became one of the first apartment hotels in the city.

The year 1928 was a big year in Oklahoma County history, because it marked the discovery of oil in this area. The ITIO No. 1, the discovery well, blew in as a gusher on December 4, 1928, at Southeast Fifty-ninth and Bryant. Discovery was by the Indian Territory Oil Illuminating Company, which later was absorbed by Cities Service Company. Oklahoma City, as the capital city and principal commercial center had benefited from oil discoveries from throughout the state, but the discovery of oil within the city created a major boom. It was barely more than a month after the discovery gusher that the surrounding landscape in Oklahoma City was completely changed. By early 1929 there were 7 other test drillings, 10 rigging up or digging, and 17 locations approved in the southeast Oklahoma City sector. The field was eleven miles long and three miles wide. It went right across the area

of the State Capitol Building. In fact, Oklahoma's became the only capitol building in the world with an oil well beneath it and derricks on the capitol grounds. The following year the depression hit the United States, but Oklahoma City grew, regardless. Oil was there and it was pumping money into the city.

However, the most dramatic Oklahoma City story was yet to come. The name of the story? "Wild Mary Sudik." It was at 6:45 a.m. March 26, 1930 that she blew in. She awoke everybody in Oklahoma City and surrounding towns. A gusher was completely out of hand. For eleven days people tried to cap her, but she ran wild. The force of the oil blew nuts and bolts in all directions. The oil shot as high as two hundred feet into the air. It even sprayed Norman, twelve miles to the south.

There were more fields to be discovered in Oklahoma County. To the north there were the Britton and Edmond fields. Still farther north was the Crescent field. These and others kept the boom going in the central Oklahoma area.

Oklahoma County, and most of the nation, started the year 1929 with a great deal of optimism, not anticipating the biggest stock market crash in the nation's history, which was only ten months away.

Montgomery Ward and Company started construction on a ten-story mail order branch and store at Main and Walker, with more than $1 million being invested. Sears Roebuck and Company completed a large portion of the remodeling of a six story grain exchange building which would house its retail store and mail order business at Grand and Harvey. General Mills announced construction of a five-hundred-thousand-bushel grain and warehouse building, after purchasing the Oklahoma City Mill and Elevator Company. A $300,000 apartment building was under construction in Lincoln Terrace. Work was underway on a new clubhouse for Nichols Hills, which had become an upscale residential suburb of Oklahoma City.

Construction projects which were announced included the new First National Bank at Robinson and First Street (now Park Avenue) and the Ramsey

The Baltimore Building on the northeast corner of Grand (now Sheridan) and Harvey.

MAJESTIC OFFICE BUILDING, OKLAHOMA CITY, OKLA.

*The Majestic Office Building on the northwest corner of Main and Harvey housed business and professional offices. One entire floor was occupied by Orban Patterson, the leader of the gambling underworld in the then-dry state of Oklahoma.*

Tower, across the street to its north, which later became the APCO Tower, Liberty Tower, City Bank Tower, and now the home of the UMB Bank.

In education, Oklahoma City University opened its new Fine Arts structure north of the college Administration Building. Its auditorium had seating for fifteen hundred, and the third floor had a lounge displaying fine paintings. The new Capitol Hill High School was nearing completion and opened in time for the school term in the fall of 1929.

Hospital construction was also underway. One building was a nurse's home at the Saint Anthony Hospital, and a second was the new Polyclinic Hospital.

A new ten-story theater and office building was being constructed downtown by Midwest Enterprises, housing the Midwest Theater on the first level. Also downtown, the Oklahoma Publishing Company built a $1.5-million mechanical unit at Northwest Fourth and Broadway.

By late 1929 the Oklahoma City oil field was flowing more than seventy thousand barrels of crude oil daily. There

apparently were no serious effects from a thirty day shutdown of production, ordered because of plummeting prices. There were 1,180 active oil operations in Oklahoma County, including producing wells. Within a seventy-mile radius of Oklahoma County there were about twenty-five hundred operations.

More federal highways were planned for the capital city. A highway from Oklahoma City to Hot Springs by way of Shawnee, Seminole, Wewoka, Holdenville, and McAlester was designated with the number 177. A highway from Oklahoma City to Del Rio, Texas, by way of Fort Sill carried the federal highway number 277.

The year 1929 was a big year for aviation. The Southwest Air Fast Express, organized by Erle Halliburton, was operating a fleet of sixteen tri-motored Ford planes passenger between St. Louis and Dallas through Oklahoma City. The line connected with other lines planned for the future, giving Oklahoma City a network of airlines in all directions. The Halliburton line later became the Safeway Line. Tom Braniff and his brother, Paul, began operating an airline from

Oklahoma City to Tulsa and Wichita Falls, Texas. In later years it became Braniff International.

That year also marked the dedication of the first Oklahoma City built airplane at the Municipal Park. This was the first plane of the Coffman Monoplanes, Inc. and made a successful test flight at the airport in the presence of eight thousand people along the field. The Coffman Monoplane offered several features in airplane construction, which had been developed by Sam Coffman. The factory was located at the former Midland Motor Company Building in the southwest part of Oklahoma City. The first plane was sold to a customer in Chickasha, and within two months a large number of orders for Coffman planes were received. Within a single month 1,582 inbound planes were accommodated on the Municipal Airport, along with 1,592 departures. Airlines included Braniff Universal, Curtis, Tibbs, and Safeway, along with private airplanes. This led to an airport bond election, which succeeded, making possible new airport facilities.

The big news nationally of 1929 was the crash of the stock market, which left some investors penniless and some workers jobless. The Depression naturally hit Oklahoma City, even though the recent discovery of oil mitigated the depression to some extent.

Several major buildings were under construction when the Depression hit the nation in 1929, including First National Bank, the Ramsey Tower, the Biltmore Hotel, and the YWCA. However, all were completed the following year. The Skirvin Tower was under construction at the time of the financial crash, and building was halted for almost ten years.

Average weekly income dropped from $25.03 to $16.73 during the Depression. At the Brittling Cafeteria you could order breakfast with fresh orange juice for ten cents and hot biscuits for a penny each. One large egg with two strips of bacon, hominy grits and ham gravy cost seven cents, but many could not afford it.

*Looking west down Main Street of Oklahoma City in the early 1930s. The tall building in the center of the picture is the Majestic Building, which was once located on the northwest corner of Main and Harvey.*

# CHAPTER VI

SURVIVING THE DEPRESSION

The 1930s opened with the coldest month Oklahoma City had ever experienced, with snow, ice, blizzards, and sub-zero temperatures. The average daily temperature for the month of January 1930 was 23.3 degrees—a record only approximated by January 1918 when the average was 25 degrees.

Immense construction was underway, despite the stock market crash only two months earlier. Oklahoma City was leading the entire South in construction, with building permits totaling more than a million dollars for the twenty-seventh consecutive month.

One of the major projects was the proposed $700,000 YWCA building. The eleven-story Black Hotel at Grand and Hudson was rapidly taking shape, as was the Biltmore, a block away. On Highway 66, the three-building Park-o-Tel was under construction. However the biggest construction projects of the year were the building of the First National Bank Building and the Ramsey Tower, across the street to its north at First and Robinson, both slated for completion in 1931.

Construction of a $3-million underground long distance telephone cable to connect Oklahoma City and Dallas was progressing. A similar project had earlier connected Oklahoma City and Tulsa. Other underground projects were planned. Construction was also underway on the third Santa Fe Station in the same location as the first two.

Word was received from Washington during the summer that the contract for the new $1.1-million addition for the Federal Building was being let, including a wing on the east and a tower eight stories high. The growing steel and tank business, enhanced by the oil boom brought expansion to two Oklahoma City companies—the Boardman Company and the American Tank Company.

Although the petroleum industry was getting major attention following the late 1928 discovery well, the city's annual business in livestock was strong, totaling more than $30 million. More than two hundred thousand people were visiting Oklahoma City every year, delivering livestock.

The distinction of staging the largest junior livestock exhibition in the world was accorded Oklahoma City when the fifteenth Southwest American Show eclipsed all previous records. In addition, the horse show sponsored by the Junior League of Oklahoma City was the largest ever held south of Kansas City and was recognized as one of the best ever to be staged in the country. To this date, Oklahoma City continues to be considered the horse show capital of the nation.

A tree planting program, sponsored by the Junior Chamber of Commerce, resulted in planting six thousand trees in the area.

During the year the new 640-acre air terminal was completed and open, with airport operations being transferred from the old field. Setting world records in the field of aviation was Oklahoma City's Wiley Post flying the *Winnie Mae*, provided by Oklahoma City oilman F. C. Hall, and christened in honor of Hall's daughter. Statewide interest was evidenced in a series of district model airplane contests under sponsorship of the Chamber of Commerce. Finals were held at the State Fair, receiving a medal offered by Wiley Post.

The Oklahoma City oil field continued to expand. The south Oklahoma City field was producing 10,000 to 25,000 barrel gushers, with no dry holes recorded. The estimated potential production of the Oklahoma City pool in 1930 was 800,000 barrels from 102 completed wells.

However, in some areas the Depression, which began with the stock market crash, was taking its effect. The Elks Lodge lost its headquarters building on the northwest corner of Northwest Third and Harvey. The Masonic bodies lost their building at Northwest Sixth and Robinson, and purchased the smaller Knights of Columbus structure, at the later site of the Murrah Federal Building.

(later Rock Island) bisected the middle of downtown, going east and west. It was followed by the Frisco only a few years later. The Rock Island depot was immediately north of where the Skirvin Hotel was later built. The Frisco Station was located in the approximate site of the present Municipal Building. Oklahoma City wanted and needed railroads in the early days, and was enthusiastically willing to cede land for the east to west tracks through the middle of downtown. By 1930, it was a severe problem. Automobiles, which did not exist when the tracks were built, were by 1930 stalled by the large number of trains crossing through downtown. To alleviate the matter with the north-south tracks, the Santa Fe constructed elevated lines. To eliminate the east-west tracks downtown, new tracks were

By 1931 Oklahoma City was beginning to feel the depression. A notice in the chamber of commerce publication suggested that citizens should not invite friends or acquaintances to move to Oklahoma City unless they have means of taking care of themselves or have guaranteed business connections. The chamber also reflected the Depression when the price of its daily luncheon was reduced from 60 cents to 45 cents.

However, new construction was continuing. The city completed its fortieth straight month of building permits totaling more than one million dollars. Principal projects were the Santa Fe Railway program of $5 million, set for the following year; Municipal Airport improvements, approved by the earlier bond issue; remodeling of the Key Building (formerly Elks Lodge); and the building of Taft Junior High School at Northwest Twenty-third and May Avenue.

The Reagan Brick and Tile Company was building a plant for $250,000 in far north Oklahoma City, near the Santa Fe tracks. The Oklahoma Club was being enlarged, and the Medical Arts Building was being remodeled. A post office was going into Capitol Hill. A five-story addition was being made to Saint Anthony Hospital, scheduled for occupancy within a year. It brought hospital capacity to 375 beds. In the entertainment area, the Coliseum in the Stockyards was being rebuilt for use in livestock shows and other events requiring large seating and display facilities. This remodeling also marked the beginning of the bi-annual Boy Scout Circus.

Church construction continued. A new organization was founded publishing church papers. It was called the Oklahoma City Church Press, later to be changed to All Church Press. One who got his start as a salesman for these papers was W. P. "Bill" Atkinson, who later was the founder of Midwest City.

A new radio station, KOMA, owned by Southwestern Broadcasting Company of Fort Worth, went on the air in September 1932. Carey Lumber

*Looking west over the tops of buildings from the Colcord Building during the 1930s.*

Oklahoma City, in 1930, had a population of 185,383, placing it in forty-third place among cities in the United States. The metropolitan population of Oklahoma City, which included all of Oklahoma County was larger than the combined populations of the next two cities of the state.

Ever since the Run of 1889, trains were running across the surface through the center of Oklahoma City. From north to south it was the Santa Fe, just east of Broadway. Within a short time, the Choctaw

being built for the Rock Island and Frisco lines in south Oklahoma City. In mid-1930 the last trains on those two lines crossed through downtown Oklahoma City, to be diverted to the new tracks to the south. In place of the tracks which were removed from the center of the city, Couch Drive was built, and within a few years the new Civic Center was constructed along the former railroad lines, including the Municipal Building, the County Courthouse, the Municipal Auditorium (now Civic Center Music Hall), the police station and jail.

Company, previously in Chicago, moved to Oklahoma City late in the year. The Carey family has played a prominent role in Oklahoma City since that time. John A. Brown of Oklahoma City and John Dunkin of Tulsa purchased the interest of Anson Rorabaugh in the Rorabaugh-Brown Dry Goods Company, and for the next forty years the John A. Brown Company was the largest department store in the city.

With its new hotels being completed, Oklahoma City in 1931 hosted 344 conventions with a total of 136,000 delegates. The city had held fourth place among all cities in the United States in the number of conventions scheduled for the following year, exceeded by New York, Chicago and Washington, D.C.

Oklahoma City sports in the early 1930s was highlighted by the Goldbug football team of Oklahoma City University. In 1931 the team won nine straight games, losing none. One of the team members was Wayne Parker, who later became president of the Oklahoma Gas and Electric Company.

Aviation continued to be a highlight of the development of the city and county. Work was well underway on an administration building for the new 640-acre municipal airport. A story on the project pointed out that the project was being handled entirely with resident labor, with no outside laborers needed—an announcement keyed to the Depression.

In the youth area, the Central Oklahoma Area Council of the Boy Scouts purchased 160 acres of land for a permanent Boy Scout camp for summer outings and weekend camps. The site is located fifteen miles southwest of Oklahoma City near Wheatland on the South Canadian River, and continues to operate, as Camp Kickapoo. The Camp Fire Girls had an active year, with their main project being a tree planting program, working with the Jaycees.

The Depression was deepening in 1933 when Oklahoma City had the second banking holiday in its history, declared by Governor William Murray. This holiday started March 22, and lasted twelve days. Various forms of script sprang up all over the state. The first holiday was declared in 1907, shortly before statehood, by acting Governor Charles Filson, in the absence of Territorial Governor Frank Frantz.

Sunday, July 22, 1933, was a significant day in Oklahoma City history, with two nationally remembered news events taking place. One was the landing of Wiley Post in New York, setting a new record for an around-the-world flight. The second event was the kidnapping in Oklahoma City of oilman Charles F. Urschel, a wealthy trustee of the estate of Tom B. Slick, "king of the wildcatters."

A 1934 report showed Harbour-Longmire to be the second largest furniture store in the United States—second only to a store in Los Angeles. This store had opened in 1920 as a furniture repair shop. Another rapidly growing Oklahoma City company was the Macklanburg-Duncan Company, selling weatherstripping throughout the world. In that year eighty-five people were employed by the company, but its sales force covered the nation.

Facilities for entertainment were advancing in the city, despite the depression. Approval was received for the Oklahoma City Municipal Auditorium. Authority was granted to proceed with completion of an outdoor amphitheater at Lincoln Park, with wooden seats provided for eleven thousand people. It was to be built by the Civilian Conservation Corps with federal funds, as part of the recovery program. A major city event, beginning the following year at the amphitheater was an annual Easter Sunrise program, which continued for many years. Next to come would be the Olympia Circus, which was the first of a series of entertainment programs scheduled for the amphitheater. Funds were appropriated by the Board of Education to assure the completion of the Taft Stadium, which was to be a sports facility serving schools throughout the city. A great deal of the money for this project was raised by the Jaycees.

*The YWCA Building in downtown Oklahoma City opened in 1930.*

This was a banner year for sports in Oklahoma City. The OCU Cardinals were named the North American champion girls' basketball team. Oklahoma City played host to the Western Golf Tournament, at Twin Hills Country Club, and the national championship golf tournament was scheduled for the following year at the same course. By this time Oklahoma City offered a choice of twelve golf courses. Polo enthusiasts could find facilities at the Nichols Hills riding academy. The Oklahoma City Tennis Club maintained a number of fine tennis courts. The city had a Texas League baseball franchise, and in 1935 won the Dixie championship.

Oklahoma City made the national spotlight in 1935 when a city newspaper executive, Carl Magee, who had headed a committee to study the automobile downtown parking problem, came up with the idea for the world's first parking meter. He commissioned an engineer from Oklahoma A&M College to design it. The first meters, manufactured by Magee's Park-o-Meter Company, were installed in downtown Oklahoma City, but the meter quickly spread nationwide. In the first year, eight thousand meters were sold, with customers ranging from

*An artist's rendering of the Amphitheater at Lincoln Park from a postcard. The Amphitheater was built during the 1930s by the Civilian Conservation Corps.*

as far away as Miami, Florida, and Meadville, Pennsylvania.

On the negative side, on August 15, Oklahoma City's worldwide aviation champion, Wiley Post, and his companion and passenger, Will Rogers, were killed in an airplane crash in Alaska on the first leg of a planned worldwide trip. Post's funeral, held in Memorial Park, was the largest attended service in the city's history.

The petroleum industry was continuing to prosper in the City. Besides the Oklahoma City field, the Edmond field had been developed to a major proportion, as was the Koetch Field north of Edmond, and the Britton field. During the year Oklahoma County led all other counties in the number of barrels of oil handled by pipeline companies, with a total of fifty-four million barrels. During 1936 Oklahoma City officials established a new drilling zone ordinance ordering regulation of the flow of oil within city limits. Governor Marland ordered the National Guard into the Oklahoma City field to keep process servers from handing out court summons ordering halting of production. As a result, Judge Ben Arnold handed down a decision declaring that city officials had no control over state land.

Commercial air conditioning surfaced for the first time in Oklahoma City in 1936,

beginning in theaters. The first theaters to install the new cooling device were the Orpheum, which had earlier been the Overholser Opera House, and the Criterion.

In the cultural area, an art gallery was established by the Works Progress Administration in the Commerce Exchange Building, under the direction of artist Nan Sheets. More than twenty-three thousand people visited the gallery during its first eight months. Another WPA project, the Municipal Building, the first of the new structures of the civic center, was completed and dedicated.

For the second year in a row, Oklahoma City was the scene of a major new invention, which played a revolutionary role in the lives of people nationwide. Sylvan Goldman, owner of the Humpty Dumpty supermarkets, developed and introduced the folding and nesting shopping cart for grocery stores, and established the Folding Carrier Company in Oklahoma City.

A major event of 1937 was the opening of Oklahoma City's new Municipal Auditorium. Reservations were made for sports events, including boxing and wrestling, as well as concerts, dances, large dinners and theatricals, as well as conventions. Also completed during the

year was the new Skirvin Tower Hotel, across the street west from the Skirvin. The year also marked the coming of a new radio station, KTOK, which brought to the area the coast to coast network of the Mutual Broadcasting System.

With Hitler rattling sabers in Europe and Japan doing the same in the Far East, the Oklahoma City Junior Chamber of Commerce offered cash, medals, and a trophy for orations by high school students on any phase of world peace.

The year 1938 brought substantial improvements to Lake Overholser by the Oklahoma City Water Department and the WPA. The new boat dock at the lake meant an added spurt to boating enthusiasm and clearance and beautifying of the lake shores. The re-vamping of the Oklahoma City Zoo, another federal project, was completed and a dedication event took place. In the State Capitol complex the Jim Thorpe State Office Building south and west of the Capitol, was under construction.

The year 1939 marked the fiftieth anniversary of the Run of 1889 and the creation of Oklahoma City. On April 22 the anniversary day of the Run, Oklahoma City had two huge '89er parades—one down Main Street and one on Southwest Twenty-ninth Street in Capitol Hill. The Oklahoma City Traffic Department estimated that about one hundred thousand people—about half the city's population—saw the pageant, portraying the city from tents to towers. The procession included prairie schooners, buckboards, cowboys on horseback, surreys, and hundreds in frontier garb. They were marching in tribute to the estimated ten thousand who camped in tents fifty years earlier on the day of the Run. The State Fair that year was centered around the anniversary and the fireworks show each night featured a reproduction of the Run.

A major business item of 1939 was the announcement of a new store opening in Oklahoma City, with Raymond A. Young as manager. This was the TG&Y store at 825 North Broadway, which was the beginning of a national retail chain headquartered in the city.

# CHAPTER VII

WORLD WAR II AND RECOVERY

Wartime and water problems hit Oklahoma City and Oklahoma County at the same time. War clouds were gathering as Oklahoma County entered the fourth decade of the 20th Century. In 1940 the city was in imminent danger of disaster from the failure of Lake Overholser to furnish sufficient water for its people. A municipal bond election of 1940 approved development of an Upper Bluff Creek Reservoir of seventy-five thousand feet of water, a new modern pumping and filtration plant, expansion of the current distribution system, and improvements at Lake Overholser.

By 1940 there was a program to widen all federal highways entering Oklahoma City to at least four lanes. Construction in several directions from Oklahoma City during 1939 had indicated that this was a project and not merely a hope. Other projects of 1940 were to complete Taft Stadium to accommodate thirty-five thousand people, to stabilize the symphony orchestra, to construct a suitable library building and art museum, and to assure Oklahoma City police and health control in areas adjacent to present city limits.

The city was growing, but not at the rate of previous censuses. In 1890 Oklahoma City had a census of 4,151; in 1900, 10,037; in 1910, 64,205; in 1920, 91,295; in 1930, 185,389; and in 1940, 204,517.

Oklahoma City was also growing in the cultural area. Annette Burford of Oklahoma City won a contract with the Chicago Opera Company in competition with many of the country's outstanding singers. The Oklahoma City Police Quartet, the Flat Foot Four, made its debut at the New York World's Fair after winning the state contest and a national competition. Starlight concerts of the Oklahoma City Symphony were held during the summer at Taft Stadium.

On the minds of all at the turn of the decade were the wars raging in Europe and in the Far East. Oklahoma City in 1940 was designated a draftee induction center, and the first group of draftees, numbering 444 men, began to arrive in late November. Whenever possible they were sent on to camp the first day. However, the city was equipped to take care of those who needed to stay overnight. The Oklahoma State Fair Association offered for this purpose the facilities of the Fairgrounds without charge, except for payment of utility bills.

Construction continued in Oklahoma County, despite wartime. Total building permits for the first ten months of 1940 amounted to $5,152,000. Downtown a new, modernistic three-story home of Harry Katz, Inc. was announced at 313 West Main.

In early 1941 work was underway on the second municipally owned airport in Oklahoma City, being constructed near Bethany at a cost of $1.5 million. The airport was completed by the end of the year. The Army then took over the first airport which, by that time, had been named Will Rogers Air Base. Commercial planes took over use of the new field, leaving the Wiley Post Field for non-scheduled flying, and the old municipal air field for the Army.

The year 1941 also brought the announcement by C. B. Warr, Oklahoma City realtor, that he would be building 122 homes on a sixty-acre tract east of the new municipal airport near Bethany. This development was inspired by the rapid expansion of the Oklahoma City aviation facilities, and marked the beginning of what would later become the town of Warr Acres. Hardly a month afterwards the War Department approved a $16 million air repair and service and supply depot four and a half miles east of Eastern on the south side of Southeast Twenty-ninth Street. By late 1941 construction was underway. It was designed to be a permanent military installation employing 3,500 civilians, with more than 300 Army personnel, and with an estimated payroll of $5 million annually.

A later bulletin from the War Department announced allocation of one of the five newly organized air support commands to Will Rogers Field. This brought to the city every type of plane and equipment used to bring about a uniformed grouping of all of the aviation elements that a ground force needed to insure the success of a mission. Within the same month Oklahoma City was named one of thirty-nine cities in the United States selected by the Civil Aeronautics Authority as an air traffic control point, where flying activities are carried on jointly by military and civilian authorities. CAA took over jurisdiction at Oklahoma City and thirty-eight other points as a matter of unifying and consolidating control of both military and civilian operations under a federal authority.

The Variety Club Health Center was also dedicated in 1941, located on South Hudson at the spot where the Main Post Office now stands. This building was operated as the Oklahoma County Health Association and the Tuberculosis Christmas Seal organization. The County Health Association served children and expectant mothers in low income families. When the building was demolished for construction of the Post Office, the two organizations split and the health association, renamed Variety Health Center, moved to a building at Southwest Eighteenth and Walker, and moved to its present site at Northwest Sixth and Walker in the early 1990s.

In September a one-hundred-pound dynamite blast heralded the start of lake construction of Bluff Creek Reservoir. Several hundred citizens were at the dam site for the event, which led to the reservoir, later named Lake Hefner, in honor of Mayor Robert A. Hefner.

The big news as 1941 was coming to a close was the bombing by the Japanese of

Pearl Harbor, and the entry of the United States simultaneously into both the European and Pacific wars. Wartime programs were to occupy the minds of virtually every citizen of the county, and with two Army Air Corps facilities, and the CAA facility, Oklahoma County was destined to play a major role. To support servicemen stationed in the area, the USO opened a facility at 431 West Main, offering conveniences and diversion, including laundry facilities, overnight bunks, a library, and a recreational hall.

Gasoline rationing and military travel greatly enlarged bus travel, resulting in the construction of a $100,000 bus depot at Sheridan and Walker.

Women would also play a bigger role than ever before, with men leaving for the Armed Forces by the thousands. For an example, it was announced that all aluminum welding work at the Douglas plant would be handled by women. The huge air transport plant being built by the War Department and operated by Douglas Aircraft Company was larger than earlier indicated, and included manufacturing as well as assembling of planes. Oklahoma City was also getting an office of government petroleum coordination. With the Forty-fifth Infantry Division on active duty, the National Guard state headquarters was converted into a training point for air depot and aircraft plant workers, leased by the War Department for $1 a year. Oklahoma City University began an educational program for war activities, including courses in inorganic chemistry, engineering drawing, industrial accounting, and statistics. Within a year its participation was given a substantial boost by being authorized to train five hundred Army aviation cadets with a program which got underway in the following year, making it a major cadet training center.

Early 1942 brought the announcement by W. P. "Bill" Atkinson that he would build a model city adjacent to the newly planned air depot. The project was scheduled to cost more than $4 million, and would accommodate some twenty-five hundred persons as civilian employees of the Midwest Air Depot. The project was to be known as Midwest City, and was given a high rating by the Federal Housing Administration. When completed, it was slated to take care of the seven thousand skilled technicians expected to be employed at the depot.

By March Colonel William R. Turnbull, commander of the air depot, established temporary offices in the Commerce Exchange Building downtown. A tent city was established adjacent to Will Rogers Field for housing eleven hundred enlisted men, due to arrive within two weeks. Because of the defense facilities located within the county, the area experienced the lowest housing vacancy in several years. The twelve-story Herskowitz Building on the corner of Grand and Broadway was scheduled to be remodeled for 76 living units by conversion of the top 11 stories. Other business buildings were under consideration to be converted into living quarters.

Patriotic activity was at its highest level. Oklahoma City, working as a unit in War Bond and Savings Stamp sales, sold in one month enough bonds and stamps to pay for the first cargo plane manufactured at the plant in Oklahoma City. The Chamber of Commerce sponsored Saturday evening social events and dances for military men stationed at Will Rogers Field.

The Rotary Club bought a $2,000 mobile canteen unit to be used by the Red Cross for service to soldiers. War Chest officials rushed detailed plans for a big war chest campaign—an expansion of the annual Community Fund campaign. The Junior Chamber of Commerce began distribution of service flags to homes in which men are in the uniformed services of their country. The Jaycees also started a project to encourage flying the American flag at homes and throughout neighborhoods. A drive was started to collect books for the military camps, using the slogan of "Victory Book Campaign." The Boy Scouts made the collection. "Victory Gardens" were promoted. Family gardens increased the homegrown supply of foodstuff in order to make available more of commercial production for the troops. Families planning such gardens were given posters identifying their patriotic efforts. The poster read, "We have a war garden."

With virtual unavailability of new automobiles in the civilian market, along with rationing of gasoline, there was an increasing dependence on mass transportation. Total revenue for the Oklahoma Railway Company in 1942 was almost double that of 1941, and for the first time in years it was operating at a profit. Automatic counters on state highways showed that traffic had decreased almost twenty-five percent in one year.

The Oklahoma City Air Depot, by now named Tinker Air Force Base for Clarence Tinker, an American Indian Air Force general killed in the Battle of Midway, continued to grow as the war progressed. In March 1943, Midwest City, adjacent to Tinker Field, held an election and voted to incorporate.

Patriotic activity on behalf of the nation's war effort and those in the service, highlighted activity in Oklahoma City. A chorus of twelve hundred school children, backed by a band and orchestra, sang patriotic music on the Oklahoma City University campus. Symphonic concerts, free to servicemen, were held each Saturday night during the summer at the Civic Center. A July 4 parade was held, with entries restricted to patriotic themes. Mayor Hefner issued a proclamation for observance of meatless month. The Oklahoma State Fair put its emphasis upon the Food For War campaign. A pick-up of tin cans for recycling was held as a part of the war effort in Oklahoma City. Raising money to replace the USS Oklahoma, sunk by the Japanese at Pearl Harbor, was Oklahoma's goal in the second war loan drive in April. The annual '89ers Day Parade was the culminating event of the campaign, which had as its goal providing $40 million for the light cruiser USS Oklahoma City. Governor Robert S. Kerr spoke at an assembly following the parade. The business and professional community of Oklahoma City held a day of prayer under guidance of ministers of the churches.

The year 1944 marked the launching from the ship building yards in Philadelphia of the USS *Oklahoma City*. Oklahoma County was joined by Cleveland County in raising $45 million in war bonds to finance the building of the vessel.

The Douglas plant was working overtime in the war effort, and in early 1944 launched an all-out, seven-days-a-week "Wings for Invasion" drive.

The year also marked the launching by air-minded Oklahomans of the Oklahoma Flying Farmers—the first all-farmer chapter of the National Aeronautics Association. This organization, established in Oklahoma City in 1944, was the first in the nation of the Flying Farmers. During the same year Oklahoma City led the nation for the number of conventions held during the year, with a total of 681. Chicago ranked second and New York City was third.

The year 1945 was a big year for Oklahoma County, marking the winding down and ending of World War II, followed by the beginning of postwar recovery. The Normandy invasion of 1944, was followed half a year later by the final German lunge, resulting in the Battle of the Bulge. This was followed by gradual movement into the heart of Germany by Allies from the West, South and East, culminating in the end of the European War. While Americans and Allies were preparing for what would have been a costly invasion of Japan, the two atomic bombings brought a sudden close to the war against Japan.

Almost immediately, Oklahoma City and Oklahoma County began moving toward a brighter future. Within two months after the close of the war, the Army announced that it would soon open Will Rogers Field to other than military aircraft. Central Airlines was granted approval for passenger and cargo air route schedules in Oklahoma. The company was later sold to Frontier Air Lines.

Approval was also received for a Continental Airlines application for direct service to Oklahoma City and Tulsa. Lieutenant General Ira Eaker, an Oklahoman who had set aircraft endurance records as a junior officer in the early

1930s, came to Oklahoma City and Midwest City to dedicate Tinker Field as a permanent Army Air Force installation.

With building curbs ending, sixty-five hundred homes were scheduled to be constructed during the next five years in Oklahoma City, which had been cramped as a result of war restrictions. The Biltmore Hotel announced a million-dollar program including a convention center. Three other hotels—the Skirvin, Wells-Roberts, and Huckins—announced major improvements. The Oklahoma Baptist Convention announced construction of a four-story building for state offices, including a broadcast studio and editorial headquarters for the *Baptist Messenger*. Four television channels were allocated to Oklahoma City by the Federal Communications Commission.

Utilities, formerly stranded by wartime restrictions, began construction programs. Oklahoma Gas & Electric Company announced a $2-million program of enlargement and modernization of the Horseshoe Lake Generating Station at Harrah, stepping up capacity fifteen percent, to seventy-seven thousand kilowatts. Southwestern Bell Telephone Company added one thousand new telephones for Oklahoma County subscribers. The installation, however, still left about eight thousand people on the waiting list.

Nine major oil companies opened or expanded offices in Oklahoma City. These included Carter Oil Company, Sohio Petroleum Company, Skelly Oil Company, Shell Oil Company, Stanoland Oil Company, Cities Service Gas Company, Fox Producers, Superior Oil Company of California, and Tidewater Oil Company.

Construction and renovation continued in 1946. The Home Theater at the corner of Northwest Sixth and Robinson, underwent a $200,000 remodeling program and re-opened in December. This replaced the Shrine Auditoriums, and was scheduled to show first run motion pictures as well as feature stage performances. It later became the *Journal Record* Building, which was severely damaged in the 1995 bombing. The Oklahoma Industries Authority

financed building of Monitor Paint Factory on West Grand Avenue and an Empire Foods building in Midwest City. A $7-million veterans hospital was approved for construction in Oklahoma City, and a campaign was started by Oklahoma Medical School alumni to raise $3 million for a medical research center, which later became the Oklahoma Medical Research Foundation.

Air travel was moving forward fast in Oklahoma County. By early 1946 Will Rogers Field, which had been a vital wartime base, once again belonged to Oklahoma City. It included 35 buildings and 5 hangars. Within two months after regaining the base, a huge air show was held on the field, with proceeds furnishing scholarships for Oklahoma youths taking Civil Air Patrol cadet training. Braniff Airlines requested new air routes connecting the Pacific Coast with Oklahoma City. A Civil Aeronautics training center was under construction.

Oklahoma was scheduled to retain its Forty-fifth Infantry Division, plus two Air National Guard fighter squadrons under the War Department's plan for a national guard of 622,000—more than twice the pre-war strength. The new Forty-fifth Division became an entirely Oklahoman organization, rather than representing four states as it was prior to the war.

However, the recovery from war restrictions also took its toll. With the renewed availability of automobiles following the war, the interurban rail service between Oklahoma City and El Reno and between Oklahoma City and Guthrie was discontinued in 1946 by the Oklahoma Railway Company. The interurban to Norman continued for awhile afterwards, but later was discontinued.

The year marked the construction of the Centre Theater across the street north from the Municipal Auditorium, which closed in the 1970s, and was remodeled at the beginning of the new century for the Oklahoma City Art Museum.

"300,000 in 1950" became an Oklahoma City slogan, as the city looked forward to the 1950 census. At that time the population of greater Oklahoma City was estimated to be 267,000, with the city limits proper being 220,000.

The major event of 1947 was the dedication of the long-planned Lake Hefner, adding seventy-five thousand acre feet of water supply, and solving Oklahoma City's critical water problem for many years. The celebration included demonstrations of a fire boat and other firefighting equipment, fly-casting, and displays of sports and vacation equipment. Lake Hefner joined with Lake Overholser in forming Oklahoma City's two reservoirs. Together they had a capacity of thirty billion gallons. The capacity of Lake Hefner was almost five times that of Lake Overholser.

In early 1947 plans were underway for a four-lane superhighway between Oklahoma City and Tulsa. It was to be financed and operated as a toll road. The plans were presented to Governor Roy Turner by Oklahoma City and Tulsa chamber leaders. It led to the beginning of Oklahoma's turnpike system, which would be the first superroad west of the Mississippi River.

By 1947 the Oklahoma City oil field, discovered late in 1928 was ten miles long, with its greatest width being three-and-a-half miles. Some 1,600 wells had been drilled—350 within the corporate city limits.

A Capitol Hill one-thousand-watt radio station, KLPR, began operation at the frequency of 1140 kilocycles. Shortly afterwards KTOW, at 800 kilocycles opened on the thirty-third floor of the APCO Building (now UMB Bank), making the seventh radio station in Oklahoma City.

An interesting event of 1947 was a contest held in the Municipal Auditorium at the close of the Oklahoma Poultry convention. It was a contest to determine the greatest rooster. The idea was to select the top chanticleer with a combination of photogenic qualities and crowing abilities. The winner replaced the rooster which gave forth in the main title of *Warner Pathe News*. The final selection was made at a performance put on in Hollywood style in the Municipal Auditorium. Movies of the event were shown all over the world.

In 1948 a multimillion-dollar highway program was approved for Oklahoma County by the Public Roads Administration. It was to be a long range program, including possible routes of major highways in and out of Oklahoma City, with cost to be divided between the state and federal governments.

Building plans were disclosed to give downtown Oklahoma City its single biggest improvements since the war. United States Fidelity and Guaranty Company was to build a three-story structure with strong enough foundation for ten stories. The Douglas Office Supply firm started a modernization program. Oklahoma Industries Authority added another thirty-five acres north of Northeast Thirty-sixth Street along the Santa Fe tracks. Oklahoma City University completed construction of thirty new buildings. Citizens State Bank, the city's newest banking institution, opened its doors for business. The Salvation Army began a $350,000 campaign for building a new headquarters building. The State Fair board approved studying a location at Northwest Tenth and May for a new fairgrounds facility.

By 1948 Oklahoma County was feathering out as a broiler raising area. The county's production that year was about 150,000 commercial boilers, averaging two and a half pounds. They were being raised principally in nine plants, with capacities ranging from 100 to 7,000 birds.

The year brought interesting events. The national conference of the Friends of the Land, meeting in Oklahoma City, participated in a special project to build a farm in a day. They took a rundown farm at the intersection of Northwest Tenth and Portland, and the Friends watched the rebuilding of the farm in one day. The rebuilding included the terracing, building of the farmhouse, soil conservation projects, and other improvements. This property later became a part of Oklahoma State University. A full-scale reenactment of the Run of '89 took place on the site that night, with one thousand horses and riders participating.

Oklahoma City also had a garden pilgrimage that year, with 2,500 garden visits being made by visitors from 31 state cities, 20 from out of state and one from London, England.

The Freedom Train came to Oklahoma City in early 1948, and was on display at the Union Station with more than ninety documents connected with American history. The year closed with a Christmas pageant at the Municipal Auditorium, with more than three thousand people turned away because of the overflow crowd.

The year 1949 brought to Oklahoma City a facility which would change, to at least some extent, the lifestyles of virtually every individual in the county. It happened on June 19, when television arrived in Oklahoma City. With the introduction of WKY-TV, Oklahoma City became one of the first cities in the Southwest to offer this newest medium to the public. Initially, Oklahomans were able to view TV three hours daily except Saturday. The station had completely equipped the Little Theater in the Municipal Auditorium, installing modern transmitting equipment. The station was equipped with a portable truck for picking up numerous athletic games and events. All programs were local, and it provided opportunities for local bands, singers and entertainment groups.

On July 3 the Oklahoma Medical Research Foundation held ceremonies beginning construction on the new building for the foundation. Guest speaker was Sir Alexander Fleming, discoverer of penicillin and a Nobel Prize winner. The building was to cost $800,000 and was to be located at Northeast Thirteenth Street east of the University of Oklahoma Medical School.

Ground was broken for construction of the $500,000 St. Luke's United Methodist Church at Northwest Fifteenth and Harvey, and for the new $500,000 home for Central State Bank at 304 Northwest First Street. Construction was underway on the first of one thousand planned houses—400 west of Nichols Hills School and 600 in the area of Southwest Forty-fourth and Pennsylvania.

*The main entrance to Frontier City shortly after its completion in 1958.*

# CHAPTER VIII

## A DECADE OF GROWTH

Final census figures released by the Department of the Census gave Oklahoma's population as 2,233,000, which was a decline of 4.4 percent from 1940. There was a large loss during the war years, but brisk gains were underway and were continuing since 1945. The official count for Oklahoma City for 1950 was 243,504, and for the metropolitan area it was 325,352. This is a numerical gain of 81,193 since 1940. In 1890 3.7 percent of the people lived in towns or cities. The 1950 census showed fifty-one percent of Oklahomans living in urban areas. Oklahoma City continued to be the largest city in Oklahoma, having approximately sixty-one thousand more people than Tulsa.

Oklahoma City building permits for 1950 hit a high, totaling more than $50 million. This was more than twice the former record year of 1929, which had $24 million in permits. The year saw building dedications for the new TG&Y stores' general office building, the new Southern Baptist state headquarters building, and the St. Ann's Home for the Aged. The C. R. Anthony Company announced building of a new corporate headquarters, and Oklahoma Publishing Company announced a major expansion, including a new press, capable of printing sixty-four-page signatures.

The Oklahoma Gas and Electric Company completed and dedicated its Rnew Mustang Generating Station south of Lake Overholser and west of Council Road. With production capability of 112,000 kilowatts, this made Mustang the largest power plant in Oklahoma. Oklahoma Natural Gas Company announced that it would construct a new $800,000 service building in Oklahoma County.

The Oklahoma Symphony signed a contract for the biggest radio series in its history, providing a world-wide audience. The thirteen-week broadcast series, originating through the Mutual outlet of station KOCY, included coverage through the Trans-Canada Radio Network, Voice of America, Radio Free Europe, and the Armed Forces Overseas Radio Network. A poll taken by *Musical America* magazine showed the Oklahoma Symphony second in popularity, led only by the New York Philharmonic Symphony.

Construction contracts increased forty-five percent in Oklahoma City over 1949. In Oklahoma City there was $36 million in new construction and engineering contracts awarded.

Bids were open for the new $2-million YMCA building, set for construction at Northwest Fifth and Robinson, replacing a building on Northwest Second Street, which later was incorporated into the Kerr-McGee complex. The YMCA building was severely damaged in the 1995 bombing and subsequently torn down.

An annual school event, starting for the first time in 1950 was the Oklahoma City Science Fair which, in its opening year, had 150 exhibits entered by Oklahoma City high school students.

The summer of 1950 brought the invasion by Communist North Korea of South Korea, resulting in United Nations support of South Korea and the immediate involvement of the United States. Four National Guard divisions were called to two years active duty beginning September 1, including Oklahoma's Forty-fifth Infantry Division. Also called were the two wings of the Oklahoma Air National Guard. Both organizations went to Louisiana—the Forty-fifth Division to Camp Polk, and the Air Guard to the air base at Alexandria.

The year 1951 brought the announcement that Midwest City had been judged America's best and most completely planned city among those with homes normally priced in the under-$9,000 bracket, winning honors sponsored by the National Association of Home Builders. There were thirty-six model communities from coast to coast competing for the honor.

An internationally acclaimed organization was born in Oklahoma City when John L. Peters, a Methodist minister, preached a sermon urging a program of self-help training and assistance for developing nations. It resulted in his organizing World Neighbors, which trains and sends people throughout the world on self-help missions. This organization, still headquartered in Oklahoma City, has played a major role in lifting forty-three countries on three continents from poverty.

Plans were approved for a new seventy-thousand-square-foot library, scheduled to get underway in 1952. It would have capacity for 750,000 books and facilities for 300 reading patrons, including an auditorium on the top floor. It would be in the same spot as the existing library, Northwest Third and Robinson.

The Aero Design and Engineering Company in Bethany, building twin-engine executive aircraft, opened for business and demonstrated its capability by flying from Oklahoma City to Washington, D.C. on one motor in seven hours and twenty-five minutes—a feat never before accomplished.

Macklanburg-Duncan, manufacturer of building items, moved from Northwest Twenty-third Street to Oklahoma Industries Authority property an Northeast Forty-first and Santa Fe. Oklahoma City's telephone system changed its dials from numbers to prefix letters with numbers.

The Oklahoma City livestock market

*A view of the campus of Oklahoma City University from the 1950s.*

ranked eighth in the nation as a leading cattle market. The Oklahoma City Better Business Bureau was named first in the nation for community service. The city's post office dispatched a record 47,000 pounds of airmail during the year, beating by far the previous record of 38,000 pounds.

In March the Forty-fifth Infantry Division moved from Camp Polk, Louisiana to the northern island of Hokkaido in Japan, to provide a security force for the island. In December the division moved to the western front in Korea for combat duty. Meanwhile Oklahoma Air Guardsmen had moved to the Far East to support the operation in Korea.

The year 1952 brought network television to WKY-TV, through the National Broadcasting Company. The public schools opened their own radio station, KOKH-FM, with studios in Classen High School.

The new four-lane Classen Avenue, greatly enlarged and lighted with a modern streetlight system, was officially opened with a huge parade featuring Oklahoma City bands, new fire equipment, commercial vehicles, and floats. The Classen project marked the beginning of a new high-powered street

light system by OG&E, replacing existing lights. A county bond issue brought about the construction of the Britton Expressway on Western Avenue from Northwest Fiftieth to Britton Road.

OG&E announced it will spend approximately $10 million on an expansion of its Mustang plant in west Oklahoma City, doubling the generating capacity and making it by far the largest power plant in Oklahoma. Kerr-McGee Company opened a laboratory at Northeast Thirty-sixth and Santa Fe, aimed at finding better methods of extracting uranium from ore. The company had earlier purchased ore properties in Arizona.

The city dedicated two fine church buildings—the Westminster Presbyterian Church at Northwest Forty-third and Shartel, and the Crown Heights Christian Church at Northwest Fortieth and Western. Meanwhile, First Presbyterian announced that it was moving from downtown to build a new sanctuary at Northwest Twenty-fifth and Western, and First Christian was building a complex at Northwest Thirty-sixth and Walker. Saint Luke's United Methodist Church, one of the largest of its denomination in the nation, was preparing for a new location at Northwest Fifteenth and Robinson.

Petroleum continued to play an increasing role in the industrial development of Oklahoma County. By the close of 1952 there were approximately thirty thousand persons working in oil and related industries in the county.

Early 1953 saw the opening of the Turner Turnpike from Oklahoma City to Tulsa—the first of the state's turnpike system.

Ground was broken in April 1953 on the most modern and one of the largest Sears Roebuck & Company stores in the country. The store was being constructed on the northwest corner of Northwest Twenty-third and Pennsylvania. For Oklahoma City it was the first move of the principal facility of a major department store away from downtown, and marked the beginning of the center of retailing being moved from the central business district. The Agnew Bridge, providing an important north-south link between Capitol Hill and downtown Oklahoma City, was completed and celebrated.

Work was underway on the new Fairgrounds at Northwest Tenth and May, which would replace the fairgrounds east of Eastern. The first phase of the building program of the new fairgrounds was scheduled to be ready for the 1954 State Fair of Oklahoma, and the entire project was set for completion in time for the semi-centennial celebration of the State of Oklahoma. Also planned was a new baseball park on the west side of the fairgrounds. Concurrently, the Black High School, with parks and playgrounds, was being built on the old fairgrounds.

Southwestern Bible College, training ministers and missionaries for the Pentecostal Church, had moved to the 4700 block on Northwest Tenth Street, and was occupying a former mule barn by 1953. Over the years the campus was enlarged with several buildings, but closed in the early 1970s. The new Gold Star Memorial Library on the campus of Oklahoma City University was opened for the fall term of 1953, with a collection of fifty-four thousand books.

Application was approved for a second Oklahoma City television station, to be known as KWTV, Channel 9, carrying programs of the CBS network. Construction began in the summer of 1953. It included the world's tallest man-made structure—a 1,580-foot antenna, which was 121 feet taller than the Empire State Building. Also approved and under construction was Oklahoma City's first UHF television station, KTVQ, to be located in the First National Building. This station lasted for only a short time before closing.

In the business community, Bendix-Westinghouse Automotive Air Brake Company opened its Oklahoma City plant at 3737 North Portland; the Terminal Building at Grand and Harvey downtown (formerly streetcar terminal) was remodeled and converted to the Globe Life and

Accident Insurance Building; and the Harris Meat and Produce Company opened a new ultra-modern plant at 1616 West Reno. An expansion of Tinker Air Force Base, including additional land acquisition, was approved by Congress.

The State Fair of Oklahoma opened at its new grounds at Northwest Tenth and May, preceded by a "Colorback" program in which the colors of the Forty-fifth Division were returned to the Oklahoma National Guard.

In early 1954 the fifty-millionth animal was marketed at the Oklahoma City stockyards, setting off a celebration by the livestock industry. It was forty-four years earlier that the first packing plant was brought to Oklahoma City. Another landmark was an American Airlines plane, in flight between Los Angeles and New York, which landed in Oklahoma City to mark the one millionth airplane to land at Will Rogers Field. Those aboard were requested to disembark for the ceremonies following the landing, and were greeted by the sixty-piece Capitol Hill Junior High School Band. Each lady received an orchid, and souvenirs were give to all aboard.

A milestone was reached at the Municipal Auditorium when the air conditioning of the auditorium was

completed. This was celebrated with a show featuring Bob Hope. Shortly afterwards color television made its debut in Oklahoma City on WKY-TV, Channel 4. Other major events included a garden pilgrimage, with attendance from throughout the state and thirty towns outside the state, and the first Soap Box Derby to be held in many years.

The Oklahoma Farm Bureau moved into its new five story headquarters building at Northeast Twenty-fourth and Stiles, and groundbreaking ceremonies took place for the new Speech and Hearing Building in the medical center on Northeast Thirteenth Street.

Construction began in 1955 on a new turnpike from Oklahoma City to Lawton, with plans to continue to the Texas line.

Early 1955 saw Oklahoma City being awarded the location of the National Cowboy Hall of Fame by trustees from the seventeen historical western states. These trustees formed the governing body of an organization that eventually made reality of one man's dream. He was Chester A. Reynolds, a homesteader in Colorado, who became a clothing salesman, and finally chief executive officer of H. D. Lee Company of Kansas City. On a visit to the Will Rogers Memorial of Claremore, he conceived the idea of an institution to

*An aerial view of downtown Oklahoma City looking northeast from an early 1950s postcard.*

recognize those who helped to develop the American West.

Labor Day weekend in 1956 saw a mammoth National Aircraft Show. An added feature was placing soil of three continents around a flag plaza to demonstrate the widespread effect on training facilities at the aeronautics center. Ultimate expansion of Aero Design and Engineering Company at Tulakes Airport was assured by civic underwriting of the costs, as the Civil Aeronautics Administration upgraded its status in the airfield.

The years 1956 and 1957 were key years for entertainment, education and tourism. For a number of years the city had been looking forward to Oklahoma's 50 years of statehood in 1957. The Semi-Centennial event at the State Fairgrounds was preceded by an earlier major function in 1956, labeled Southwest American Exposition, and carrying the theme, "Arrows to Atoms." Youth were lured to the exposition by the slogan, "Meet me at teen town."

Oklahoma's Semi-Centennial year got a noisy and colorful start January 18 with a

*Looking east on Main Street from Hudson from an early 1950s postcard. The skyline includes the Hightower, Halliburton, and Hales Buildings.*

large downtown parade of bands, round-up clubs, Indians and other participants, climaxed by a public bonfire of Christmas trees. The Exposition at the fairgrounds from June 14 to July 7 was the main attraction of the year. Eleven nations made it the largest trade fair of the Southwest. It included an exhibit from the Soviet Union, first to come to the United States from that country since the 1939 World's Fair. Exhibits included total involvement from twenty-two nations.

The U.S. Postal Department cooperated by issuing an "Arrows to Atoms" commemorative three cent stamp on opening day. An International Symposium of Science, Industry and Education was a highlight with leading figures of this and other countries as speakers. A "Boomtown" reflected some of our more gaudy heritage. Composed of old-style buildings, it portrayed an Oklahoma oil boom town of an earlier period.

Broadcasting his NBC television show throughout the period of the Semi-Centennial was Dave Garroway, host of the show. Mickey Rooney and others of national stature performed in stage appearances, which took place in the grandstand each evening. On July 7, 1957, a time capsule was buried at the fairgrounds to be opened in the year 2007, which would be the end of the first century after statehood.

Jimmy Burge, who had been director of the Oklahoma Semi-Centennial Exposition, had eyed Boomtown as the possible centerpiece for an amusement park, and before the close of the celebration, he had decided he would build such an attraction. At the close of the Semi-Centennial, an auction was planned, in order to dispose of those attractions which would not become a permanent part of the State Fair of Oklahoma, and Burge decided to cast his bid for Boomtown. Assuming no one else would want the old-style frame buildings, he decided to make only a modest sealed bid. However, to his surprise, he found himself outbid by Mrs. Perkins of the

Perkins Fence Company. However, this did not stop him from building Frontier City. He constructed it in grand style, with its own pioneer buildings as a centerpiece, and opened it a little more than a year later. Having changed hands and been enlarged several times, Frontier City became the cornerstone for Premier Parks, which owns many amusement parks nationwide, including Six Flags over Texas, and which is ranked in size second only to the Walt Disney Company.

A major institution coming to Oklahoma City in 1958 was Central Christian College of Bartlesville, a Church of Christ-sponsored institution, which changed its name to Oklahoma Christian College before moving to far north Oklahoma City on the Edmond border. The college conducted a three-day Freedom Forum for the Oklahoma City area business community shortly after its move, featuring speakers of national repute. Within two years it was conducting forums and seminars over a several state area, designed principally for youths of high school age.

In November it was announced that Mr. and Mrs. John E. Kirkpatrick were donating $267,000 for a $400,000 Oklahoma Art Center, also at the fairgrounds. Later they provided $40,000 for the Science and Arts Foundation Building nearby. An airport improvement bond issue for $7,497,000 was passed by voters.

Early in 1958 a new plant for Continental Plastics was indicative of yet another step in man-made products rather than fabrication of natural materials. Security Federal Savings and Loan Association opened its new quarters on Northwest Second and Harvey. A new downtown institution of the Bank of Mid-America took over the old Baum Building, vacated when Fidelity moved to Park Avenue and Harvey. In August 1960 Mid-America was absorbed by Liberty National Bank. On the northwest Highway near Tulsa Avenue. Wedgewood Village was under construction as an amusement park, in competition with the long established

Springlake Park. Wedgewood survived a number of years. In March Dr. Jack S. Wilkes became sixth president of Oklahoma City University. Later he would be mayor and still later, until his untimely death, president of Centenary College in Louisiana.

Toward the end of the first quarter of 1958, Tinker Field held contracts for a new base hospital. The first four phases of the Oklahoma City floodway, to keep the North Canadian under control, were completed by the middle of 1958. In April ground was broken for the Atoka reservoir, a distant, but needed adjunct to the city water system.

Announcement was made for a new federal building, to be a block long and five stories tall, on Northwest Fourth Street just north of the Post Office and Federal Building on Third Street. Before year's end a research building for the University of Oklahoma Medical Center on Northeast Thirteenth Street would be underway. The George Fredrickson Field House on the Oklahoma City University campus was dedicated.

The year also marked the construction of the first hospital outside of the downtown area. The Baptist Memorial Hospital at 3300 Northwest Expressway was built at the city's highest point and was constructed with $4.6 million in private funds.

The final year of the decade was a big one. To protect Will Rogers Airport from encroachment and mitigate problems faced by many cities, civic leaders underwrote $300,000 to secure 500 acres on the approach patterns, to be repaid later by bond issue funds. On Southwest Fifteenth Street a major cross-country truck terminal was put in by Transcon Lines. Now called the Federal Aviation Authority, the installation at old Will Rogers Field took over control of the nation's air space. It had a permanent payroll then of 1,875 persons. A $153,000 grant from the parent FAA in Washington aided the city in improving Tulakes Airport, later Wiley Post Airport. After a rather disastrous fire in June 1959,

*A lighted oil derrick adds color to this night scene north of the Oklahoma State Capitol in the 1950s.*

Wilson and Company constructed a new and more modern plant at the stockyards which, after Armour closed its plant, became the only major packer in the city, although there were a number of independents. A major shopping area, completed in 1959, was that of Penn Square, north of the Northwest Expressway east of Pennsylvania Avenue. This center of 7 large buildings contained 48 retail stores and a restaurant, including the largest Montgomery Ward retail store in the nation at that time. The center was located to the west of Belle Isle and the Belle Isle power plant.

An Oklahoma Air National Guard building program on the northwest section of Will Rogers Field was underway in September. Many temporary World War II buildings were removed. A long-awaited and needed structure across the North Canadian River was dedicated in the Agnew Street Bridge. October of 1959 saw OG&E making a third enlargement of its Mustang power plant, the largest generating plant in its system. For its achievements in traffic safety, Oklahoma City for 1959 was awarded four certificates in varied classifications by the National Safety Council. This was the only city in the nation to receive that many awards, and tied with Grand Rapids, Michigan, for top place among all similarly sized cities.

*The Oklahoma Heritage Center at Northwest Fourteenth and Robinson was once the home of the former Oklahoma City Mayor and Oklahoma Supreme Court Justice Robert A. Hefner.*

# CHAPTER IX

BUSINESS ORGANIZATIONS EXPAND OUTWARD

February 1960 saw the first mobile library service in the city. What was termed a $44-million "luxury home and country club project," surfaced with announcement of the Quail Creek residential development and country club in northwest Oklahoma City. In the area east of Lake Hefner, another major area development, Lakehurst, included 375 homes. Earlier this had been part of the G. A. Nichols estate.

The U.S. Army Reserve began construction of an armory at May and Reno. Ground was broken for two state office buildings north of the Capitol, later named the Sequoyah and Will Rogers Buildings. Oklahoma Industries Authority sold its last piece of property in the

Willow Springs area to Frigiquip Company. Construction was underway on a $2-million Federal Reserve Branch Bank at Northwest Third and Harvey.

The National Cowboy Hall of Fame by this time had been an empty shell atop Persimmon Hill in northeast Oklahoma City. In order to keep the Western spirit alive until funds to finish the structure could be obtained, its leaders conceived the beginning of an annual Western Heritage Awards program, to include awards to writers, publishers, composers, and performers in the field of Western lore. The first event was held in the spring of 1960 in the Persian Room of the Skirvin Tower Hotel, with James Garner as master of ceremonies. It has been held

every year since, and the event was moved to the Cowboy Hall itself after the museum was opened. This annual event has probably brought more national celebrities to Oklahoma County than any other activity. It played a major role in keeping the spirit of the Cowboy Hall alive and in the final raising of funds for completion.

Early in 1961 part of the long planned Southwest Seventy-fourth Street Expressway was under construction. It would link Interstate 35 with the announced Southwestern Turnpike, later named the H. E. Bailey Turnpike.

In May, by gubernatorial and mayoral proclamation, the first week was proclaimed "Fly the Flag Week." Leader in this promotion was Lee Allan Smith of WKY-TV, who later was backed by the Oklahoma City Association of Broadcasters in the creation of the annual "Stars and Stripes" extravaganza, which brought nationally known celebrities to Oklahoma City for patriotic programs.

Lone Star Brewing Company, purchasers of Progress Brewery, spent about a million dollars in renovating that plant. A new banking facility—State Capitol Bank—opened at Northeast Thirty-eighth and Lincoln, with a totally modernistic style and floating air lobby. It is now Arvest bank.

The newest form of visual entertainment—Cinerama—a three-dimensional form of motion picture, came to Oklahoma City in 1961, appearing first at the Cooper and Warner Theaters. In sports entertainment, the Oklahoma City Indians Triple-A baseball farm team of the Texas Rangers, gained a new name—the Oklahoma City '89ers.

In May 1961 ground was broken for Elm Creek Reservoir, a detention lake which had a dual purpose. It protected the south approach to Tinker Field runways and was terminus of the Atoka pipeline, bringing water to the city distribution system. Aero-Commander, later to be a property of the Rockwell interests, rolled out its first turbo-jet executive airplane in May. It would sell for $600,000, as a basic price, and cruise at more than 500 miles an hour. Cato Oil and Grease Company, near the former fairgrounds, had a disastrous fire and rebuilt a new facility to produce products sold throughout the nation and to other countries. Later the company was purchased by Kerr-McGee. In June the FAA placed its aero-medical research in Oklahoma City, which resulted in an added facility for the FAA Center. Across the city another defense installation came into being with the Thirty-second Air Defense Command of the U.S. Air Force. An illustration of the international importance of the FAA Center was provided in mid-1961 by the fact that 327 representatives of fifty countries received training in the city.

Of lasting value to the city and state, although not measurable, was existence and use of a "host family" visitation program which permitted foreign visitors to spend time with a city family. In the fall of 1961 it was noted that Oklahoma County, small in area by comparison with most others counties in the state, had more impounded water than any other county, with 11,065 acres of surface water.

In September, Oklahoma State University opened its Technical Institute in Oklahoma City, an adjunct to the Stillwater campus. This institute offered evening courses, in addition to day programs in technical skills below degree level, available to local residents and others. With bond funds for right-of-way purchase, the city laid out its share on forty-nine miles of expressway as part of a $60 million new highway development.

Comedian, dancer and serious musician Danny Kaye helped to get 1962 off to a good start in January by appearing with the symphony at a benefit performance. After many years in a downtown hotel, the Oklahoma Press Association moved to a home of its own on North Lincoln. Announcing additional construction were United Founders Life Insurance Company for a twenty-story circular building near North May and the Northwest Expressway; Kerr-McGee for a similar sized office building in its growing center; Oklahoma Publishing Company for a $2-million, five-story structure between the original, ornately trimmed building on North Broadway and the mechanical plant on Northwest Fourth Street. The city was already basking in another "record" year summing up for 1961 with $219,531,092 in capital expenditures.

The State Fair of Oklahoma added 117,000 feet of new building space, primarily in the livestock area, including housing for a "children's barnyard," with mothers and offspring of many animal types. Tinker Field, in 1962, was selected as a site for an automatic switching system for Air Force logistics.

The decade saw the integration of Black and White races in housing and in use of facilities. Schools had been integrated by federal court ruling in the previous decade. The early 1960s saw the beginning of the "sit-in" movement, with Blacks occupying seats in restaurants and other facilities in which had been closed to them. Arrests for breaking the law took place, but the movement resulted in changing of laws which had allowed the restrictions. In many ways Oklahoma County and Oklahoma led the way in the integration process.

A major industry coming to Oklahoma City in 1962 was the General Electric Company in far west Oklahoma City, manufacturing electronic equipment. This facility was destined to grow over the years, but to change ownership on three different occasions.

The Sheraton-Oklahoma Hotel, formerly Biltmore, had a $1.5-million interior "face-lifting." Partly to honor the chain which was to operate the hotel for several years, Grand Avenue had its name changed to Sheridan, pronounced almost like Sheraton, but supposedly honoring the general who once commanded troops in western Oklahoma. The city council also renamed Northwest First Street Park Avenue and Northwest Second Street Robert S. Kerr Street.

Cain's Coffee Company built a new $2-million plant on the Broadway Extension south of Edmond, while Macklanburg-Duncan had $1-million expansion on North Santa Fe.

The year 1963 was just starting when United States Senator Robert S. Kerr died. Services at the First Baptist Church drew President John F. Kennedy, Vice President Lyndon B. Johnson and a host of other dignitaries. Kerr, the first native born Oklahoma governor and developer of a major fuels industry, was called the "uncrowned king of the Senate" because of his power there.

Developers announced a $15-million, enclosed shopping mall project to be built on the original Shepherd homestead on Northwest Twenty-third Street east of Villa. First called Shepherd Plaza, the name was changed to Shepherd Mall. There were 70 retail stores within the mall project, which encompasses 54 acres. The Federal Reserve Branch Bank acquired an addition downtown. In March 1963 more than 350,000 county residents received Saulk oral vaccine as part of the national drive to eliminate polio. Mid-America Life Insurance Company erected a $1.2-million headquarters on North Lincoln. A drive to obtain $750,000 for support of Mummers Theater was successful. This was matching money for a $1.25-million grant from the Ford Foundation.

Exploring the concept of a "Tivoli Gardens," similar to that of Copenhagen, for a downtown urban renewal area, the director of that world famed installation was brought to the city for a presentation at the Chamber. A local committee visited Denmark to see the original complex in April 1963.

Something new was added to the mail addresses as the city received a zip code prefix of 731 on July 1, 1963. Old zone figures were to be added to the prefix. A tennis center on the Oklahoma City University campus emerged, bearing the name of Travis Kerr Magana, a son of Mr. and Mrs. Cecil Magana and grandson of Mr. and Mrs. Travis Kerr, following a $75,000 contribution. Dan James sold the Skirvin and Skirvin Tower Hotels to the Statler Hotel Corporation. A federal grant of $936,000 for improvements at Will Rogers Airport was matched by the Oklahoma City Airport Trust.

The year 1963 marked the beginning of the Lyric Theater, a performing arts organization which has played a major role in the cultural life of Oklahoma City ever since its organization.

In early fall, the world's largest combined cycle generating plant was dedicated at Harrah by OG&E. It combined the use of gas jet and steam pressure in a single generating unit, adjacent to Horseshoe Lake. That month also saw dedication of the Belle Isle branch of Oklahoma City libraries. KOCO-TV put up a new transmission tower on Britton Road, east of North Kelley. KWTV also carried out a major expansion.

As 1963 neared its end, the Oklahoma National Stockyards Company could brag that it hosted the "world's largest feeder and stocker cattle market." Virgil and Henry Browne announced that the Oklahoma Coca Cola Bottling Company would place a 127,000-square-foot facility on ten acres across from the fairgrounds on North May. Plant capacity would be eighteen hundred bottles per minute.

The city's seventy-fifth anniversary came in 1964, basking in afterglow of another "record year" when $317,970,310 was committed for growth. On the anniversary of the Run of 1889, instead of a rifle shot, there would be a sonic boom, which Stanley Draper insisted was the sound of the future. The Urban Renewal program officially opened in this anniversary year with clearing of areas near Northeast Thirteenth Street and Lincoln Boulevard for new and relocated medical establishments. The State Fair planned improvements on two buildings and erection of a monorail to support a new type of ride over the grounds. Oklahoma Industries, Incorporated added a third structure to the General Electric industrial complex in the northwest area. The water supply of Oklahoma City was enhanced by the completion of the new Lake Stanley Draper south of the city.

Star Manufacturing Company started construction on a $1-million plant on a twenty-acre site near Interstate 35 and Southeast Eighty-ninth Street. At Northwest Sixth and Hudson, Continental Apartments were rising as the city's first high rise downtown apartment structure.

To dedicate the Fourteen Flags Plaza at the State Fair, President Lyndon Johnson came to the city. He provided some amusement to spectators, and concern to Secret Service agents, when he climbed aboard a saddled horse nearby and put on an exhibition of neck reining.

George Shirk, then-mayor of Oklahoma City, as well as president of the Oklahoma Historical Society, brought a stronger appreciation of history to Oklahoma City.

One of his early projects was to form a history-oriented committee to develop an official seal for Oklahoma City. He also appointed an Oklahoma City Historical Preservation Commission, giving commission members the challenge to mark historical structures and locations and to accept neighborhood applications for historical designation, which required the Commission's approval for outward changes of appearance. After his term as mayor, and until the final months preceding his death, Shirk served as a member of the commission.

Oklahoma Medical Research Foundation added a $1 million addition to its facility on Northeast Thirteenth Street. A new building was dedicated at the FAA Center to house national aviation records, for which responsibility was transferred to Oklahoma City.

The year 1965 was a banner year for Oklahoma City because it marked the grand opening of the 130,000-square-foot National Cowboy Hall of Fame and Western Heritage Center. Long hampered for lack of money for completion, the shell of the building stood high, unfinished, and empty on top of Persimmon Hill near the intersection of Northeast Sixty-third and Eastern. The spirit of the Hall had been kept alive through the annual Western Heritage Awards each spring, which brought national celebrities in communicating the story of the Great West through motion pictures, television, and books, but the people of Oklahoma were awaiting the opening of the museum. It was eventually completed as part of a bond issue through the Oklahoma City Chamber of Commerce, and its opening in the summer of 1965 was a major event for the city and county. Western motion picture star John Wayne led the dedication parade in downtown Oklahoma City, which included some of the best known riding groups and Western attractions in the nation. This was the first national tourist attraction to be located in Oklahoma City, and brought visitors from throughout the world. Within three years it would bring in a million visitors.

The opening of the National Cowboy Hall of Fame attracted into Oklahoma City a major national event—the National Finals Rodeo. This event, often dubbed "The World's Series of Rodeo," brought in the cowboys nationwide who had achieved the largest number of victories or near victories during the rodeo season to compete for the national championship. The event remained in Oklahoma City for several years until lured away by the large purse which could be offered by Las Vegas.

A sporting tradition—ice hockey—returned to Oklahoma City in 1965, after a thirty-two year absence. The team, called the Oklahoma City Blazers, played in the newly completed Jim Norick Arena at the State Fairgrounds.

The year 1966 marked the dedication of the new Oklahoma City Post Office at Southwest Fifth and Harvey. Moving into some of the vacated space in the former Post Office was the United States Customs office, following the recent selection of Oklahoma City as a new location.

A children's zoo, with friendly animals for petting was opened at the Oklahoma City Zoo.

Dedicated at the close of the year was the new four-level, 200,000-square-foot terminal for the Will Rogers World Airport. With this opening, Oklahoma City, with a 10,000 foot and 7,200 square foot runway, both designed for future enlargement, became the world's first airport specifically built to serve faster-than-sound aircraft. Braniff Airways announced a one-stop flight to New York City and Central Airlines began its Dart service, including Enid, Ponca City, Stillwater, and Dallas.

The Oklahoma City Municipal Auditorium, which had been closed several months for remodeling, was re-opened early in the year, to be rededicated with a new name—the Civic Center Music Hall. This was the first remodeling since 1954, when minor changes were made to the 1930s building and air conditioning was added.

A major sporting event coming to Oklahoma City during the year was the national softball championship tournament, attracted because of the relocation of the International Softball Association to the city and the planned International Softball Hall of Fame and Museum, planned for the Lincoln Park area.

Another event coming to Oklahoma County in 1967 was the Festival of the Arts, which was destined to become an annual event, attracting artists and visitors from a wide area. Entertainment in the first year's festival included the Oklahoma City Symphony, the Oklahoma City Junior Symphony, the Mummers Theater, Civic Ballet Junior Corps, the Junior League puppets, a brass quintet, a duo piano team, and choruses and concert bands from area schools.

U. S. Post Office, Oklahoma City, Okla.

*The first major building to house the U.S. Post Office in Oklahoma City opened early in the century on Northwest Third between Harvey and Robinson.*

A highlight of the State Fair of Oklahoma was a Japanese exhibit covering twenty-one hundred square feet. Redesigned for electric operation at the fair was its popular monorail. The Howard Johnston hotel at 5301 North Lincoln was enlarged. The newly formed Oklahoma Industries Authority secured its first industry—Meco, Inc., a branch of a company headquartered in Wichita, Kansas. The company made latex products, household latex, and other rubber products.

In other industrial programs, LSI (Lear Sigler) added 30,000 square feet to its facility, CMI Manufacturing Company added 190,000 square feet, and American Body and Trailer Company announced a million dollar production plant to double its output. A new university hospital facility was leading the way for Oklahoma City's medical center to work its way east of downtown.

Newly organized in 1967 was the Oklahoma City Junior Achievement program, designed to teach young people about free enterprise and how the business system operates.

The year 1968 brought the retirement of Stanley Draper, executive vice president and chief operating officer of the Oklahoma City Chamber of Commerce, after forty-eight years with the Chamber. Draper is recognized by many as the principal builder of Oklahoma City. The Stanley Draper Expressway (I-40 through the city) and the Stanley Draper lake, then under construction, were named in his honor. Replacing Draper as head of the Chamber staff was Paul Strasbaugh.

Central High School, which opened in 1910 as Oklahoma High School, saw its last graduating class in 1968. In more

*The home office of Standard Life and Accident Insurance company once occupied the former home of lawman, oilman, and developer Charles Colcord at 421 Northwest Thirteenth Street. The house was later removed.*

recent years, the historic building was purchased by Southwestern Bell to become its state headquarters. The east foyer of the building was developed by the Oklahoma City/County Historical Society and the Central High School Alumni Association as the Central High School Museum.

The Oklahoma City Zoo is a popular attraction for the people of Oklahoma County as well as throughout the state, but the zoo added to its popularity with the initiation of a zoo walking safari, providing visitors the opportunity to walk through with a staff guide.

By this year Oklahoma City had redevelopment pains. The Urban Renewal program was growing nationally, and civic leaders of Oklahoma City wanted to be a part of it. An Urban Renewal Authority was organized, and plans were made to replace old with new structures.

The Tivoli Gardens in Denmark were a known attraction, and a delegation from Oklahoma City went to Denmark to study its design. They came home with excitement, wishing to develop similar gardens in Oklahoma City. To begin the project, the city commissioned construction of a giant floral clock in the Civic Center park, across from the music hall.

Meanwhile major companies were announcing construction of new buildings. First was Fidelity Bank, which had been at the Park and Harvey location only a few years, after moving from the Baum Building. Fidelity announced it would construct a new office building between 15 and 20 stories. Kerr-McGee followed shortly afterwards, announcing the McGee Tower, to cost $15 million and to be 30 stories high. The big announcement came one month later when Liberty National Bank announced a thirty-five-story building south of the Skirvin Hotel, which would become the tallest building in the city. All three of these structures would replace older existing buildings, so demolition of buildings was quickly underway.

In other business expansion, away from downtown, Celluponic Systems, Inc. a subsidiary of Mosinee Paper Mills constructed a plant at 317 East Hill, manufacturing a new method of mulching vegetable crops with continuous coils of paper; American Trailers broke ground for a new facility and Northwest First and Morgan Road. Diamond Crystal Salt Company opened a fifty-eight-thousand-square-foot facility, making and distributing food specialty items. Fred Jones Manufacturing Company expanded its plant.

In the field of education Oklahoma Christian College University broke ground for a $400,000 American Heritage Building and Oklahoma City University began a $6-million capital campaign for campus expansion.

A 1968 bond election passed, releasing $115 million to be spent for thirteen areas of city improvement.

General Electric moved into its new 108,000-square-foot facility at Morgan Road and Reno in early 1969. In other events of the year, construction began on Lincoln Plaza, one mile north of the State Capitol. This facility would include a wholesale market, along with an office and hotel center.

In March Firestone-Dayton announced selection of Oklahoma City as the location of a new tire manufacturing company, to be located at Southwest Twenty-ninth and Council Road. Within weeks afterwards, ground was broken for the new CMI plant. DeLuxe Check Printers announced location of a plant during the summer.

In late summer the Fleming Company announced it would move its headquarters to Oklahoma City from Topeka, Kansas. Fleming would later become the nation's leading wholesaler or grocery products, and in the year 2000 moved its headquarters to Texas. Another major company moving its headquarters to Oklahoma City from Chicago was Wilson and Company, one of the nation's two largest meat packing companies.

Urban renewal downtown was continuing. First National Bank was enlarging its headquarters to the east. The Skirvin Hotel, purchased by the H. T. Griffin Company, was being remodeled, with a ballroom being added to its north. City National Bank, anticipating the completion of the new Liberty Tower, announced that it would move into the former Liberty National Bank Building.

The big construction project at the close of the decade was breaking ground for a new convention center, later to be known as the Myriad.

Incorporated for the first time was Oklahoma City Beautiful, an organization promoting litter abatement, planting and landscaping. Spearheaded by Stanley Draper, Sr., this organization had its beginnings as the beautification committee of the Oklahoma City Chamber of Commerce in the early 1960s.

*A night view of the Bicentennial Plaza, looking east from an upper story of the Civic Center Music Hall.*

# CHAPTER X

## THE URBAN RENEWAL PERIOD

The 1970s began with breaking ground for the International Softball Association headquarters and the National Softball Hall of Fame and Museum in Lincoln Park. The National Cowboy Hall of Fame acquired and restored the *End of the Trail* statue, which had been deteriorating in a park in California ever since winning the sculpture award for James Earl Fraser at the Pan American Exposition nearly forty years earlier.

Urban renewal was on the move. Many buildings went down, drawing criticism from some, because of the historical significance of some of the structures.

Parking was upgraded. The construction of two large parking garages was getting underway. One was the Santa Fe Parking Garage, on E. K. Gaylord north of Main Street. The other was the Main Street Parking Garage on the north side of Main between Broadway and Robinson.

Another major downtown project was a $4.8-million central cooling and heating

plant by Thermal Systems, Inc., located between Main and Sheridan near the Santa Fe tracks. It was designed to serve downtown businesses.

Reaching completion was the new, modernistic Mummers Theater. The Mummers had organized as an amateur theater group in 1949, with its early productions in a retired circus tent. Attaining popularity. It advanced into old buildings converted into theaters, until attaining a major grant from the Ford Foundation for construction of a theater building. The upkeep of the large, modern building, which was not designed for multiple uses, appeared to be more than the theater group could handle. Within a year and a half the theater organization closed. Later it became the home of the Oklahoma Theater Center.

Motel space was on the increase. Lincoln Plaza opened a mile north of the State Capitol on Lincoln. Trade Winds

Motor Inn opened with 204 rooms at Eastern and Reno, and land was purchased for another at I-40 and Rockwell.

The economy was growing. The Hertz Corporation announced that it would locate in Oklahoma City with a one-hundred-thousand-foot building on the Northwest Expressway near Lake Hefner.

Conoco announced a six million dollar plant in south Oklahoma City, employing 125 people. Trammell Crow Company purchased 236 acres at the southeast corner of I-40 and Meridian for speculative industrial use. Ralston-Purina announced a plant for manufacturing pet food on a thirty-seven-acre site in the Santa Fe Railway Industrial District at Broadway and Memorial Road. The National Foundation Life Insurance Company began construction on its third high-rise office building on the Northwest Expressway at Grand Boulevard.

In the governmental sector, FAA began construction on a $6.3-million,

200,000-square-foot building. It would house the Coast Guard Institute, an aircraft accident investigation school and computer services. East of Tinker Air Force Base a Navy and Marine Corps reserve training facility was under construction.

The year 1971 saw the purchase of the John A. Brown Department Store by the Dayton-Hudson Company, which continued operation under the John A. Brown name. This was the oldest, and, at one time, largest department store chain in the state of Oklahoma, having been formed near the time of statehood as the Sydney Brock Store.

Oklahoma State University dedicated its new Oklahoma City campus at 900 North Portland, south of the state fairgrounds. This technical institute was organized as a division of the university's college of engineering. The university started an extension program in Oklahoma City in 1961, and it gradually grew in size and popularity until a campus of its own was needed. Since establishing this campus, enrollment has increased and new courses have been offered.

Scrivner-Bogaart constructed a new seventy-five-thousand-square-foot structure at Southeast Fifty-Ninth and I-35, and Hereford Heaven, a division of the Hormel Company, built a fifty-six-thousand-square-foot structure at 7300 Southwest Twenty-ninth Street. Construction was underway on a new 350,000-square-foot warehouse for TG&Y. Haggar broke ground for a new manufacturing and distribution site at Southwest Fifty-fourth and Portland. First National Bank opened a drive-in facility just north of City Hall downtown.

Presbyterian Hospital announced that it would move from the midtown to the fast-developing medical center, purchasing for its location the southeast corner of Northeast Thirteenth and Lincoln. Mercy Hospital opened its first two hundred beds in far northwest Oklahoma City on Memorial Road. The Veterans Administration Medical Center developed a $2.9-million program, including building additions and modernization of existing space and equipment.

The historic home of Oklahoma City's former mayor, Robert A. Hefner at Northwest 14 and Robinson, donated by the family to the Oklahoma Heritage Association for its headquarters, had its grand opening in early 1972. In addition to displaying the antique furniture and household items once owned by the Hefners, the home also had displays in its remodeled third story, pictures, busts, and historical vignettes of the men and women who have been inducted into the Oklahoma Hall of Fame since its inception in 1926. Through gifts from the Hefner family, C. R. Anthony, B. D. Eddie, and others, the building was enlarged to its west, to include a galleria for art exhibits, a library for study and meetings, a chapel for small weddings, and outdoor gardens for social events.

The annual Independence Day Stars and Stripes show of 1972 was telecast over NBC, resulting in an audience of more than forty million.

The long-awaited Myriad Convention Center downtown was completed and dedicated, and the Oklahoma City Chamber of Commerce moved into new offices at 1 Santa Fe Plaza, beneath the newly-completed parking garage. Also completed and opened downtown in 1972 was the new Fidelity Plaza, decorated on its outside by a large metal sculpture. The Liberty Bank and Kerr-McGee towers were under construction.

A business which began in Oklahoma City and now serves nearly half the states in the nation was Hobby Lobby, specializing in hobbies and crafts. An entertainment attraction starting that year, which has remained successful and popular, is Ballet Oklahoma.

Spring brought with it the construction of a six-story tower and pedestrian tunnel at St. Anthony Hospital. General Motors announced that it had acquired 436 acres of land adjacent to Tinker Air Force Base, but would not announce plans. Dayton Tire began a $14-million expansion. Fife Manufacturing Company, an instrument control guide manufacturer established in 1939, began a ninety-six-thousand-square-

foot-expansion. Kodak broke ground for a marketing center at United Founders Plaza. Star Manufacturing Company dedicated a new three story office building—the first three-story building in the new design it had developed. Aero-Meridian Corporation announced a seventy-thousand-square-foot office tower in the Reno-Meridian industrial district. Southwestern Bell began construction on a new thirteen-story Pioneer Building at Northwest Third and Broadway, and began face-lifting its adjoining buildings.

An annual campaign which began in 1972 was the Allied Arts Drive, benefiting the Symphony, the Art Center, performing arts groups, and other organizations, which promote the cultural life of the community. Construction began on a pedestrian tunnel connecting fourteen downtown buildings in Oklahoma City. Interconnected were office buildings, hotels, banks, shopping areas, and the Myriad Convention Center.

The Myriad hosted the National Hockey League Leafs, transferring to Oklahoma City from Tulsa.

The early 1970s brought a first to the city when Patience Latting, who had been serving on the City Council was elected mayor of Oklahoma City. Her elevation to this position made her the first woman ever to be elected mayor of a major city in the United States.

The biggest news southside in 1974 was the opening of Crossroads Mall, a regional shopping center on a ninety-seven-acre plat. Its cornerstone businesses were John A Brown, JCPenney, Dillard's, and Montgomery Ward.

In the far north sector, Mercy Hospital completed its new facility on North Memorial, with four hundred all-private rooms, while in the developing medical area northeast, the Dean A. McGee Eye Institute was under construction.

Xerox announced building of a $70-million plant on 103 acres at I-40 and Mustang Road. A new soft drink canning company was announced by Great Plains Coca Cola. Rockwell International expanded its airplane manufacturing facility in Bethany.

Construction of a building which would gain international attention because of an unforeseen future disaster was underway at Northwest Fifth Street between Harvey and Robinson. It was to be named the Murrah Building in memory of the late prominent Federal Judge A. P. Murrah.

The year 1975 saw completion of the $8-million-plus remodeling of the Skirvin Hotel, including a ballroom to its north and a tunnel across Broadway to the Skirvin Tower. Anticipating the move of the City National Bank to the former Liberty Tower, the Spaulding and Slye Company, which had acquired City National's former structure on the northwest corner of Main and Broadway, planned remodeling of the structure and enlarging it northward to the alley between Main and Park Avenue. This building had initially been the Tradesman's National Bank, constructed in 1920 and the additional space to the north, replacing the former City National Bank drive-in, once was the location of Oklahoma City's first multi-story masonry building, dedicated in 1890.

At this point Oklahoma City was looking to the nation's Bicentennial, and banker Jack Conn was appointed chairman of the Oklahoma City Bicentennial Commission. A workshop, bringing together nearly two hundred Bicentennial leaders and participants, was held at Oklahoma Christian College with national chairman Senator John Warner as principal speaker. A Bicentennial medallion with historic design, was unveiled in November.

Opening in the summer of 1975 was Kerr Park a twenty-six-thousand-square-foot park at Kerr and Broadway. The park included a pond with island for performances and a small amphitheater.

Shortly after the opening of the Bicentennial year was the arrival of the Bicentennial Wagon Train, which was crossing the nation to conclude its journey in Philadelphia—the site of the Declaration of Independence. Its arrival in Oklahoma City was celebrated with a public barbecue dinner and entertainment at the state fairgrounds. Within two months came the arrival of the Freedom Train, crossing the nation with artifacts of American Heritage, attended by thousands throughout the state during its five day stay, including school children from hundreds of schools.

The major Oklahoma City Bicentennial project was the construction of the Bicentennial Plaza in the Civic Center park east of the Civic Center Music Hall. Artifacts in the plaza included a bronze casting of Laura Fraser's bas relief sculpture of the Run of '89—the only casting ever made of the plaster carving, located in the National Cowboy Hall of Fame. The plaza also included red granite structures on which were carved pictures illustrating the history of Oklahoma City, along with vignettes of history beneath the illustrations. The dedication, on April 15, 1976, was highlighted by the burying of a time capsule, to be opened in 2007—Oklahoma's Centennial.

Opening near the close of the year was the Oklahoma Center for Science and Arts at Eastern and Northeast Fifty-second. It became known as the Kirkpatrick Center, recognizing its principal donor—John E. Kirkpatrick. Recently opened in the same area, and popular among visitors, was the Oklahoma Firefighters Museum, operated by the Oklahoma Firefighters Association. It included the small log cabin which had been the first fire station in Oklahoma Territory, constructed by soldiers at Fort Supply in 1869.

Another museum attraction opening at about the same time was the Forty-fifth Infantry Division Museum, occupying a former stone National Guard armory building on Northeast Thirty-sixth east of Eastern. The museum highlights the military history of Oklahoma, and is open for visitors daily, manned mostly by volunteers. At the National Cowboy Hall of Fame, the gigantic mounted Buffalo Bill statue, created by sculptor Leonard McMurray, was dedicated.

The year 1977 brought the opening of the new Sheraton Century Hotel, barely a block from the Myriad, with 410 rooms. General Motors announced construction

*Oklahoma City Community College.*

of its new Oklahoma City plant, expected to employ up to five thousand people. It was to be similar to one for which ground was broken in early 1974, but was deferred two months later because of an economic turndown. The factory would be capable of building up to 75 automobiles per hour on a two-shift basis, producing a total of 1,200 cars daily.

The Fleming Companies announced construction of a $15-million food center on Northeast Memorial, one mile west of Broadway Extension. The plant would include nine acres under roof.

Ground was broken during the year for a new one thousand car metro parking garage on Robert S. Kerr across the street from the Oklahoma County courthouse building. Hertz Rent-a-Car added 112,000 square feet to its facility on the Northwest Expressway.

Going down from explosives and wrecking ball was the Biltmore Hotel, which was opened in 1930 and had witnessed some of the most important meetings in Oklahoma City.

A new attraction at the State Fair was a historic Victorian style house, moved to the fairgrounds from 211 Northeast Fourth Street and donated by Jim Fentriss of Fentriss Sound.

The year 1978 was a big year for television entertainment, because two UHF stations went on the air—KGMC-TV, Channel 43, and KOKH-TV, Channel 25.

By 1979 the city was already looking forward to the coming Diamond Jubilee of Statehood, and G. T. Blankenship was named chairman of the event for the Oklahoma City area.

The year 1979 brought about Larry Jones' founding of Feed the Children, a worldwide charitable organization providing food in areas of disaster and need.

*Rose State College, which opened in 1970 as Oscar Rose Junior College, was renamed in 1983 for the long-time former superintendent of the Mid-Del School District.*

# CHAPTER XI

## THE OIL DOWNTURN DOESN'T STOP PROGRESS

The Census of a new decade showed Oklahoma County with a population of 568,933.

The beginning of the decade did not stop the building of new shopping centers continuously farther away from downtown. Opening in 1980 was Quail Springs Mall, on the north side of Memorial between May and Pennsylvania. The mall included more than 140 retail shops, and was anchored by the John A. Brown Company, Dillard's, Sears-Roebuck, and JCPenney.

As a result of new attractions of the previous decade, Oklahoma City and Oklahoma County had become an area of nationwide attention. They included the National Cowboy Hall of Fame, the Omniplex, the Oklahoma City Zoo, the Firefighters Museum, the International Softball Hall of Fame and Museum, the Harn House '89er Museum, Frontier City, the Oklahoma Historical Society and State Museum, the Oklahoma Art Center, the Oklahoma Museum of Art, the Oklahoma Heritage Center, Springlake Fun Park, and the Forty-fifth Infantry Division Museum. The Oklahoma Air and Space Museum in the Kirkpatrick Center opened in 1980.

Also opening shortly afterwards was White Water, a twenty-three-acre water theme park, brought by Silver Dollar City. This park, in addition to its water facilities, included two 18-hole miniature golf courses. Construction included enough concrete to cover a football field four feet deep. It had its own wells, and was designed to filter two hundred thousand gallons of water every four hours. It used two tons of chlorine per week for water sterilization and another two tons per week of caustic soda to neutralize the acids produce by chlorine. It had four acres of astroturf carpet.

Still to come among local attractions were the International Photography Hall of Fame, Enterprise Square, USA, and the Bricktown Canal.

Oklahoma City Beautiful began a project to plant twenty-five thousand trees above the number normally planted during a year.

The Will Rogers World Airport was undergoing a $22-million expansion, as the city projected a 139 percent increase in passenger travel in the next two decades. The expansion included a five-level garage, doubling the number of parking spaces, and a radar control system to serve the entire metro area.

In mid-June 1981 Oklahoma City began its celebration of the Diamond Jubilee of Oklahoma Statehood. Jack Conn, who had headed the Oklahoma City Bicentennial Commission, was state chairman. The celebration events were to take place for seventy-five weeks, extending through the close of 1982—the Diamond Jubilee year.

Completed in time for the Diamond Jubilee were the Myriad Gardens, a four-square-block downtown cultural and recreational park. It included a 3.5-acre lake, a 300-seat amphitheater, multi-level walkways, and a bridge. Planned for the future was the enclosed "Crystal Bridge," which was to be 275 feet long and 70 feet wide.

Opened in 1982, the International Photography Hall of Fame in the Kirkpatrick Center had moved to Oklahoma City from Santa Barbara, California. The Oklahoma Historical Society opened the

Overholser Mansion at Northwest Fifteenth and Hudson as a historical home for touring by the public. The National Cowboy Hall of Fame acquired John Wayne's collection of personal artifacts.

A new semi-annual attraction was the Paseo Arts Festival. This area, west of Walker and between Northwest Twenty-eighth and Thirtieth Streets, started in the late 1920s as a "Spanish Village," highlighted by the El Charito Mexican restaurant and the enclosed Paseo Plunge swimming pool. In the early 1970s it deteriorated into a gathering place for drug users, but was cleaned up to become an art center, with studios and shops in the late 1970s. The festival included displays and sales of arts and crafts, as well as food booths and free entertainment.

The major attraction to open during the year was Enterprise Square, a $10-million, 60,000-square-foot educational attraction interpreting the American free enterprise system. It was constructed by Oklahoma Christian College on its campus at 3501 East Memorial Road.

The American Bus Association's 1982 listing of the nation's top events of the year included two from Oklahoma City—the National Finals Rodeo and the Oklahoma City Arts Festival. Oklahoma City was one of only seven cities in the United States with two attractions listed among the top one hundred.

Beautification and planting was underway on Lincoln Boulevard north and South of the State Capitol, renamed the State Capitol Park.

The late 1970s and early into the 1980s marked a boom period for the oil industry, and Oklahoma was prospering. Many were investing, and some were over-borrowing to profit from the boom. A sudden downturn in the oil boom brought disaster to many, and Penn Square Bank, which had been a heavy lender, and had sold many of its loans to out of state banks, failed. This had a major impact upon Oklahoma, and even upon some banks in other states. However, it did not stop progress in Oklahoma City.

Construction of the largest of the new buildings downtown—Leadership Square—was begun in 1983. It was designed with two towers, one 17 stories and the other 22 stories. Also under construction was a training annex for the FAA center, designed to house flight simulators. The former Shrine building at Northwest Sixth and Robinson, more recently occupied by insurance companies, was acquired by the *Journal Record* Publishing Company, and remodeling was underway. This building was destined twelve years later to be severely damaged by the Murrah Building bombing. Farther north, at Broadway Extension and Britton Road, the new headquarters for the Benham Architectural and Engineering Company was nearing completion. To its south, Oklahoma Publishing Company was developing a site to become its new headquarters. Brixton Square, a complex of retail shops and offices was underway on the Northwest Expressway.

The early 1980s saw the opening of the Museum of the Unassigned Lands by the Oklahoma County Historical Society (now the Oklahoma City/County Historical Society. The Society had been organized in the late 1970s to preserve and transmit to the public the history and heritage of Oklahoma County. For several years the Society had been collecting historical artifacts of the area. The opportunity to open a museum came when the Society was offered rent-free space in the Melton Company building, overlooking Broadway Extension from the east, south of Northwest Fiftieth Street. The museum operated for several years, free to the public, until major cutbacks took place in the Melton Company. At the time of this publication, the artifacts are in storage, but many will later be displayed in the new State History Center, which is under construction.

Hospitals were also being improved. Mercy Health Center, on Memorial Road, was a adding a four story outpatient facility and physicians' condominium building, and Hillcrest Hospital was undergoing major expansion.

Construction was in progress in 1985 on the first phase of a corporate park—a

$400-million, 50-acre office and mixed use development north of Memorial Road and West of May. During the same year the Mid-America Bible College opened at 3500 Southwest 119th Street, moving to Oklahoma City from Houston.

The county's newest visitor attraction was Aquaticus, which opened at the zoo in 1986. It included an aquarium on its lower level and a covered grandstand above, facing a pond and a dolphin show. By this time the 180-acre zoo featured in a natural setting more than 750 species of wildlife, including more than 4,000 specimens of mammals, reptiles, birds and marine life.

A major business transaction of the year was the purchase of the TG&Y chain, headquartered in Oklahoma City, by the McCrory Company.

Following its successful campaign to legalize pari-mutuel horse racing, construction was underway in 1986 on Remington Park, scheduled to open its racing season in 1988.

The year 1987 marked the completion and dedication of the McGee Creek Reservoir southeast of Atoka, providing the city forty thousand acre-feet of water per year. It also marked completion and dedication of the softball Hall of Fame stadium, destined to host world championship tournaments.

A new annual event was Opening Night, sponsored by the Arts Council of Oklahoma City. This New Years Eve celebration includes musical entertainment, stage performances, and dancing throughout the evening in business and public buildings downtown. It climaxes with midnight fireworks celebrating the beginning of a new year. An alternative to New Year's Eve drinking parties, liquor is not allowed, and children are encouraged to come, with crafts and entertainment designed specifically for the younger set.

By this time the communities of Oklahoma County, as well as the other six counties opened by the Run of 1889, were preparing the Centennial of that historic event. A competition, conducted by the Oklahoma City Chamber of

Commerce in 1988, won by Brent Johnson, created the official emblem of the Centennial—a horse and rider superimposed over an outline map of Oklahoma. Many organizations were conducting their own centennial projects.

A major event was a parade in downtown Oklahoma City on April 22. At the same time, the annual Festival of the Arts was in full swing, also commemorating the birth date of Oklahoma County and of the other counties in the Unassigned Lands. Admiral William Crowe, an Oklahoman, then chairman of the joint chiefs of staff, was grand marshal for the parade. The city of Edmond, well-known statewide for its annual Independence Day Parade, used the Centennial as a principal theme of its 1989 event. The State Fair of Oklahoma opened with a special program, highlighting the Centennial of the Run. Aerospace America saluted the one hundredth anniversary with the Blue Angels participating as a special attraction.

But the biggest event during the Centennial year was the Olympic Festival—a preparatory event for the Olympics and the premier sporting event in the nation. The new aquatic center at Oklahoma City Community College, one of the five top such facilities in the nation, opened in time for the water events of the Olympic Festival. Oklahoma City also hosted the NCAA divisional amateur wrestling championships.

The centennial year marked other major highlights in Oklahoma County. A major portion of the Broadway Extension, connecting with I-35 and I-40, was renamed the Centennial Expressway. Groundbreaking took place for the Kilpatrick Turnpike traversing northern Oklahoma City. The Lake Hefner Parkway West Bypass and the future outer loop remained priorities. Tinker Air Force Base announced a $400-million construction program, including facilities for the new Navy E 6-a Aircraft, for which the Midwest City air base had been given responsibility. Smart Park, a new business park, opened just outside the gates of Tinker. South Community Hospital opened a $3.4-million Oklahoma Cancer Center, and Healthsouth Rehabilitation Center opened a facility near downtown. A new $4.5-million improvement program began for the horse and livestock building on the Oklahoma State Fairgrounds. It included new horse stalls and renovation of the show barn. The national Clown and Laughter Hall of Fame opened in the Carriage Hall at the Fairgrounds. Construction began on the new County jail, costing $45.7 million.

In the business area Spaghetti Warehouse acquired the former Await building for an Italian restaurant, opened at the close of 1989. This opened the door for the former warehouse district, soon called Bricktown, to become a most popular eating and entertainment spot for Oklahoma City.

Other business construction included opening of Charlie O's, which made soda fountains; enlargement of the Cardinal Paper Company; and opening of a manufacturing and assembly operation.

*The library of the Oklahoma City Community College, which opened as South Oklahoma City Junior College in 1972.*

*The Alfred P. Murrah Federal Building following the events of April 19, 1995.*

# CHAPTER XII

APPROACHING THE END OF THE MILLENNIUM

The last decade of the twentieth century began with announcement by Xerox Company of a $45-million expansion, including the manufacturing facility for a new developer chemical for Xerox copiers.

The Oklahoma City/County Historical Society began its annual Pathmaker Award program in May 1990, proclaiming the one hundredth anniversary of the founding of Oklahoma County. Living Pathmakers honored that year were W. P. "Bill" Atkinson, Jack Conn, Harvey Everest and John Kirkpatrick. Honorees from the past were E. K. Gaylord, Henry Overholser, Angelo Scott, and Nan Sheets. Luke Robison was honored for his leadership in restoration of the historic Round Barn in Arcadia.

The Sales and Marketing Executives International inaugurated its International Academy of Achievement in business, with initial honorees including the AMWAY founders, JCPenney, and Robert Funk, founder of Express Services. Pictures and achievements of these and subsequent honorees are displayed at Enterprise Square, USA, on the Oklahoma Christian University campus.

Oklahoma City Beautiful began its annual Penny Roundup for Wildflowers, raising money for planting on public grounds in Oklahoma County.

In the business community the Governair Corporation expanded its facility. Unit Parts, which rebuilds auto starters and alternators, added twenty-one-thousand square feet. Fred Jones enlarged on Northwest Thirty-ninth Street; and Normac Foods, a supplier of beef patties for McDonalds built a 122,000 square foot structure. Tealridge Manor in Edmond opened a $10-million retirement community, owned by Oklahoma Christian University.

*The Bible Building on the campus of Oklahoma Christian University.*

The year 1991 marked the move of the International Finals Rodeo and the coming of Navy air contingents to Oklahoma City. Announced for construction in downtown Oklahoma City was a new ten-story IRS building, immediately north of the Colcord Building. A $12-million expansion began on the Baptist Hospital. An election to approve a temporary sales tax aimed at bringing the United Airlines headquarters to Oklahoma City succeeded, but Oklahoma City, despite being one of the top contenders, did not gain the facility, so the tax did not take effect.

An organization, known as Capitol Domers, was created in early 1992 with the goal of raising money to place a dome on the State Capitol, as it had originally been designed. The dedicated group worked diligently toward their goal, although it would be almost ten years before it would seriously become an Oklahoma project.

The former Mummers Theater downtown, by then called Stage Center, was reopened after renovation, by the Arts Council of Oklahoma City. The National

Collegiate Athletic Association conducted its wrestling tournament at the Myriad. The Festival of the Horse, held at the State Fairgrounds, was the Oklahoma event listed in the American Bus Association's top one hundred events in the nation.

The Downtown Airpark announced an expansion involving a new thirty-one thousand-square-foot hangar. Orbit Foods expanded its operation and moved from Choctaw to a former Safeway headquarters in Oklahoma City, manufacturing tortillas, nachos, and tacos for sale to retail outlets. The newly formed API Enterprises opened a plastics manufacturing facility in Oklahoma City.

Mayor Ron Norick initiated Oklahoma City's largest public building project in its history when, in 1993, he formed the Metropolitan Area Planning Task Force to establish priorities for major proposed projects. This resulted in the MAPS proposal for a one cent temporary sales tax for building an arena, baseball park, library, and a downtown canal. Other improvements included remodeling the Myriad, Civic Center Music Hall, and some buildings on the State Fairgrounds. The election was successful. During the same year another election was held for a county-wide one cent sales tax for thirty-six months for bringing a new Defense Finance and Accounting Service Center to be located on a site near Tinker Air Force Base. Voters approved the tax by a seventy-two-percent margin, but the proposal was rejected by the Defense Department.

The year 1994 marked the first annual spring fair and livestock exposition.

A downtown business building at 123 Park Avenue, once headquarters for C. Harold Brand Realty Company was given to the Chamber of Commerce by Mr. Brand's widow, resulting in remodeling and a move by the Chamber.

Hobby Lobby broke grounds for a new 540,000-square-foot facility at Southwest Forty-fourth and Council, to be completed in 1995. It became the largest operation under a single roof to be constructed in Oklahoma City since the completion of the

General Motors assembly plant. Other enlargements included a $4-million distribution center for Pepsi-Cola, and expansion of Worldwood Industries in far southwest Oklahoma City. TeleService Resources began expansion of its Oklahoma City facility.

An important item of good news was that Tinker Air Force Base had escaped the Defense Department's closure list, once considered a threat.

However, on the tragic side, the city suffered the most severe act of terrorism ever experienced in the history of the United States up until that point in time.

April 19, 1995, began in a positive tone. The annual prayer breakfast downtown was held in the Myriad, bringing together the business and civic community in an always friendly, but serious event. Shortly afterwards—at 9:02 a.m.—a downtown explosion occurred, which could be heard, not only throughout Oklahoma City, but as far away as Guthrie and Chandler. The explosion was at the Murrah Building, a federal office structure located in the downtown area. Immediate concern was for the wounded. Help began pouring into the area within the first hour. Bodies of those killed, along with men, women, and children who were badly wounded, were carried from the building by policemen, firemen, and volunteers who had been trained for such rescue missions. Both the National Guard and the Air Force Reserve, called units to active duty to provide security and perform other missions.

Volunteers from fire and police departments from throughout the United States came to Oklahoma City to help, and some remained for a long period of time. Hospitals prepared emergency rooms and other facilities to accept and begin treating the seriously injured as quickly as possible. Churches throughout the city opened their doors and their assembly rooms to receive families of those who were missing. They remained open day and night to relay information and to provide counseling for those in grief. Some

*The Lake Hefner Streak, a bike race sponsored for many years by Oklahoma City Beautiful to benefit building of walking and bicycle trails.,*

churches kept kitchens open to feed both families within their buildings and to deliver meals to workers at the bomb site. Many restaurants did the same, refusing reimbursement for meals.

Of those killed, some bodies were covered by stone and debris, and it was several days before all could be uncovered. In all, there were 168 known deaths. There was a suspected 169th death, due to an additional, unidentified body part. One of the victims was a volunteer nurse who was crushed by falling building parts while she was participating in a rescue effort.

Another thousand people were injured—some very seriously. Most of those killed and injured were in the Murrah Building at the time of the explosion. Others were in surrounding buildings, including, in particular, the YMCA building to its north. Some were in automobiles, driving by the building at the time of the explosion.

Among those killed and seriously injured were young children in daycare centers in the Murrah Building and in the YMCA Building.

The greatest damage came to the Murrah Building, which was virtually destroyed and un-repairable. However,

there was also damage to nearly six hundred nearby buildings, many of which had to be removed. Some buildings were in limbo at the time of this publication, seven years later.

While rescue and recovery efforts were being made, police and FBI were alerted to find how the explosion came about and who was the perpetrator. It was soon found that a Ryder rental truck filled with explosives, made from fertilizer chemicals, and driven adjacent to the building, had caused the damage.

Who had committed the crime was not immediately known. Because of the earlier explosion at the World Trade Center in New York, along with terrorist activities overseas, many immediately suspected the explosion was created by Middle Eastern terrorists. One who appeared suspicious was detained at an Eastern airport where he was about to make an overseas flight. However, it was soon ascertained, almost by accident, that the crime was created by an American military veteran who had developed anger against the United States government. Only a short time after the explosion, a man by the name of Timothy McVeigh driving on Interstate 35 without an automobile license, was stopped. Because a gun was seen beside him in

*The Oklahoma City National Memorial.*

COURTESY OF J. D. MERRYWEATHER.

the front seat, he was taken, on suspicion, to the county jail in Perry. Follow-up investigation appeared to link him to the crime, and the next day, he was formally arrested.

Investigations later showed that he had become bitter with the United States government, particularly about the Waco standoff with the Branch Davidians in which those in the standoff died in a burning building. Coincidentally, and most likely intentionally, the Murrah bombing took place on the anniversary date of the Waco tragedy.

The investigation also uncovered McVeigh's research in creating explosives

from chemicals found in fertilizer, his purchase of a large quantity of fertilizer, his earlier visit to the Murrah site, and his rental of the Ryder truck involved in the explosion. Implicated with McVeigh was Terry Nichols, who had participated with McVeigh in the bomb making process and was affiliated with him otherwise.

Colorado was chosen as the site for the Federal Court trials of McVeigh and Nichols, because it was felt it would be difficult for them to get unbiased trials in Oklahoma. Eventually both were convicted in separate trials. McVeigh was sentenced to death and Nichols to life imprisonment. McVeigh was later

executed and Nichols' conviction was still on appeal at the time of this writing.

The Murrah Building bombing and its aftermath had, and continue to have a major impact upon Oklahoma City. Many of the damaged buildings have been replaced. Others were repaired and remodeled. Several churches at or near downtown received damage. Those with the greatest damage were St. Joseph's Catholic Church to the west of the Murrah Building, the First United Methodist Church to its east, and Saint Paul's Episcopal Cathedral, to its northeast. The Methodist and Catholic churches were unusable for more than three years, and were heavily remodeled. They were two of the oldest churches in Oklahoma City, and were the only two churches remaining on grounds owned by the church since the city's beginning.

The YMCA Building was badly damaged, and finally torn down. To solve the problem of new YMCA facilities, the Oklahoma Publishing Company donated its historic former headquarters building at Northwest Fourth and Broadway to the organization, which remodeled it and added a new building to its east.

The *Journal Record* Building, to the north and west of the Murrah Building, was almost equally damaged. After considerable study, it was slated for renovation, to include, among other things, a bombing memorial museum.

A task force was named by Mayor Ron Norick to consider a suitable memorial, and to develop programs to prevent further acts of terrorism in the United States. Included were a number of committees, which were considering design, preservation of archives, fundraising, and other challenges.

The site of the Murrah Building was selected for a memorial, and northwest Fifth Street was closed between Harvey and Hudson. With the assistance of Oklahoma's Congressional delegation, arrangements were made for the memorial to be known as the Oklahoma City National Memorial, operated by the National Park Service.

An international design competition was held, and the winner was the team of Hans and Toney Butzer with Sven Berg from Germany. The design included a long, shallow, rectangular pond, with 168 chairs, lighted from within, representing the 168 people killed in the bombing. The large entry wall on the east carried the large figures "9:02" (the time of the bombing) and the wall on the west carried the figures "9:03" (one minute later). The National Memorial was dedicated on April 19, 2000—five years following the bombing. Remodeling of the *Journal Record* Building followed, and

*The eastern wall of the Oklahoma City National Memorial.*
COURTESY OF J. D. MERRYWEATHER.

the museum was dedicated February 19, 2001. Ever since the period of the bombing, visitors to the site placed items on the surrounding fence, with notes expressing compassion for those killed, injured or suffering loss of a family member or friend. Artifacts were stored and many are in the museum.

Another institution which came about as a result of the bombing was the Institute for the Prevention of Terrorism, a federal institute, headed by General Dennis Reimer, an Oklahoman who had recently retired as Army chief of staff.

A Gateway Beautification Project began in 1996, including tree planting at I-40 and I-44. Beautification was a

major effort during that year, and a beautification task force, including a number of different organizations, was formed. America Online opened a support center in Oklahoma City, anticipating employment of one thousand within two years.

The Ninety-Nines, a women pilots organization founded and headquartered at Will Rogers World Airport, announced that it had more than 6,000 members from 35 nations.

Western Wireless Company, parent company of Voice Stream Wireless, invested $44 million in Oklahoma City, creating 120 local jobs in launching the new service. CIT Group Sales Financing added more than 250 employees to its Oklahoma City servicing facility.

The Presbyterian Health Foundation announced it would begin construction on a 137,000-square-foot, five-story building on the Oklahoma Health Center Research Park.

The MAPS program was showing results as 1997 came to a close. The new Bricktown Baseball Park, named for a major contributor, Southwestern Bell, was completed. Construction was ready to begin on the new Arena south of the Myriad. When it appeared that the sales tax money for the MAPS project was not going to be enough to finish the entire project, an election was held to extend the tax an additional six months to assure its completion. The people of the city, satisfied and impressed with the completed baseball park, readily approved the extension. By mid-1999, the canal was finished. It has been a popular spot for boat rides. Soon afterwards, remodeling and enlargement of the Myriad Convention Center was completed. Under construction was the enlargement of the Civic Center Music Hall, and construction was well underway on the new arena. The last major building project downtown—the new library and learning center—was completed in 2003.

The MAPS project attracted new private financing in downtown Oklahoma City. Most visible is the modern Renaissance Hotel, across the street north of the Myriad and west of Broadway, which has a skywalk from its third floor into the second level of the convention center. The remodeling of the Civic Center Music Hall played a role in attracting the Oklahoma City Art Museum into acquiring the former Center Theater northeast of the Hall, and remodeled and enlarged it for a new museum location, which opened in 2002.

The Bicentennial Plaza, built in 1976 to honor the nation's two-hundredth birthday and to spotlight the history of Oklahoma City, had suffered from city

*The interior of the Crystal Bridge in the Myriad Gardens.*

neglect, and with lights burned out or destroyed, the walled-in structure had become a haven for vagrants. The initial plan was to take down the walls and to move the historical granite panels to Bricktown. However, largely through the efforts of the Oklahoma City/County Historical Society, plans were changed to redesign it at the same location in the park (named Bicentennial Park in 1976), landscaped and lighted, but without panels. This makes this spot the cultural center of Oklahoma City, representing the visual arts, the performing arts, and the history and heritage of the area.

In 1998 Young America Corporation announced it would open a consumer care center in Oklahoma City, employing six hundred. Williams-Sonona selected Oklahoma City as a site for a new center, creating 200 positions for telephone sales, along with 600 seasonal jobs. The Hartford Financial Services Group announced opening of a customer service and sales center in Oklahoma City.

On the downside, as Oklahoma County approached the millennium, a major tornado struck on May 3, 1999, which swept across the north side of Moore, brushed the south side of Oklahoma City, and brought considerable damage to Del City and Midwest City. Even at the time of this publication, some of the damaged structures were still awaiting repair.

*Looking northeast at the Myriad Gardens, amphitheater, and Crystal Bridge in downtown Oklahoma City.*

# CHAPTER XIII

## ENTERING A NEW MILLENNIUM

For about three years citizens of Oklahoma City, as well as much of the rest of the world, were anticipating with mixed feelings the coming of the new century. Living in a computer age not even imagined a century ago, they faced warnings about lights going out, elevators stopping suddenly between floors, and banks virtually unable to operate when the midnight hour hit on December 31. For months, those involved with computers—particularly utility companies and banks—were working overtime to meet an anticipated crisis.

In Oklahoma City the Millennium was celebrated with the traditional Opening Night celebration downtown. However, its promoters were taking no chances. Elevators in the garages and public buildings were shut down at 11:30 p.m., just to be safe. However, midnight came off without a hitch, and so did the days that followed. A few people received bills and checks dated 1900,

and some were for unbelievable amounts, but, all in all, the problems were minimal.

The end of the century marked the five year anniversary of the bombing of the Murrah Building, which killed 168 people, injured a thousand, and either destroyed or damaged to some extent several hundred buildings. On April 19 the Oklahoma City National Memorial, marking the fifth anniversary of the worst act of internal terrorism in America's history, was dedicated. The three churches, most affected by the bombing, were fully remodeled and in operation. Most of the damaged buildings were repaired or replaced, but some remained closed. However, ten months after the Memorial dedication—February, 2001—the bombing museum opened in the former *Journal Record* Building, with President George W. Bush as speaker.

The year 2000 was a bad year for weather in Oklahoma City. Most of the summer was unseasonably hot and dry,

following spring and early summer rains, and early winter brought the worst sleet and ice in many years.

Oklahoma City, like the remainder of the country, was shocked with energy problems, which resulted in large gasoline price increases, followed by nationwide natural gas shortages, which, combined with an extraordinarily cold winter, brought about tremendously high gas bills.

On the plus side, people of the city had much to celebrate. In 1999 the women's basketball team of Oklahoma City University won the national women's championship, and in 2000 the OU football team, unexpectedly to most, captured the national football crown. While what appeared to be a slight recession in the year 2000, bringing cutbacks in employment by some of the larger firms, the city continued to acquire new companies. The people of Oklahoma City appear optimistic as the state approaches its one hundredth birthday.

*An aerial view of Tinker Air Force Base in the 1950s.*

# SHARING THE HERITAGE

*historic profiles of businesses, organizations, and families that have contributed to the development and economic base of Oklahoma County*

SPECIAL
THANKS TO

D&L Real Estate
Investment Company

The Joullian Foundation

# ATLAS PAVING COMPANY & METHENY CONCRETE PRODUCTS

Four companies involved in the central Oklahoma building market reside in one Oklahoma City office located at 3800 Northwest Eighth Street. The four companies have a common heritage in their principle founder and patriarch, Hugh M. Smith. Today these organizations are known as Atlas Paving Company, Atlas Asphalt Products, Metheny Concrete Products, and Materco, Inc. The story of these companies and their chief founder are typical of the often-maligned American dream and philosophy of devotion to God, hard work, dedication, integrity and family loyalty.

Hugh Smith was born to William H. and Ruth Smith in 1923 at home on the family farm outside the southwestern Oklahoma town of Roosevelt. He lived and worked on the family farm with his older brother, Walt, through the depression era and graduated high school in 1941. After serving in the Army Air Corps as a bombardier and flight officer on a B-29 Bomber during World War II, Hugh returned to Roosevelt, Oklahoma and in 1945 married his high school sweetheart, Melba L. Vaught.

Aided by the Veteran's Education Bill for college students, Hugh attended then Oklahoma A&M in Stillwater, Oklahoma. With his new wife, they set up home in the veteran's village and both worked part-time as Hugh studied Civil Engineering. After four years Hugh received his Bachelors of Science degree in civil engineering and graduated with honors in 1949.

Layman and Sons Construction Company of Tulsa hired Hugh upon graduation as materials and project construction engineer.

He quickly learned the paving industry working on jobsites around the state for the heavy road construction company. After two years with Layman's, Hugh's skills and abilities caught the attention of other employers in the Oklahoma market.

Charles Makins, owner and president of the Makins Sand and Gravel Company, had been in business in the Oklahoma City area since 1907 originally as a lumberyard supplier. Makins had become the first ready mix concrete supplier in Oklahoma County in the late 1930's. Makins was now ready to expand into the asphalt paving business. He persuaded Hugh, with his wife and two children, Debra and Bruce, to move to Oklahoma City and supervise the installation

*Above: Charles H. Makins, founder and president of Makins Sand and Gravel Company from 1907 to 1956.*

*Below: Makins Sand and Gravel Company operated the first concrete delivery trucks in Oklahoma, c. 1935.*

and operation of a hot-mix asphalt plant and paving operation in 1953.

Both concrete and asphalt operations prospered under Hugh's guidance and in 1956 the paving company was separated into Atlas Paving Company. Hugh had moved up quickly within the organization and was manager of both companies at the time of Charles Makins untimely death that same year. Harold Sherod, son-in-law of Makins, became president of the companies and with Smith continued the operation of the companies. In 1961 a major reorganization of ownership and leadership occurred. The Makins estate was sold with Smith and Sherod owning equal parts. The concrete company was renamed Makins Concrete Company with Sherod as president and Smith as vice-president. Atlas Paving Company remained intact with the officer roles reversed.

The companies continued to grow and prosper over the next decade. Makins

*Top, left: A wedding picture of Hugh M. Smith and Melba L. Vaught, 1945.*

*Top, right: Hugh S. Smith, president of Atlas Paving Company from 1961 to 1987, and president of Makins Concrete Company from 1974 to 1987.*

*Below: The Makins Asphalt Plant erected by Hugh Smith, 1953.*

expanded to six plant locations with fifty ready-mix delivery trucks. Atlas Paving was making its mark in the concrete and asphalt paving industry and installed a new hot mix asphalt-manufacturing plant in 1968. In 1974 Harold Sherod retired from the business and sold his stock to Paul Smith (no relation to Hugh). Hugh and Paul continued as equal partners with Hugh as CEO and president, and Paul as a silent stockholder.

Bruce L. Smith, the son of Hugh Smith, like his father attended Oklahoma State University in Stillwater, Oklahoma and majored in Civil Engineering. Bruce earned a Bachelor of Science degree in 1975 and a Master of Science in Civil Engineering in 1976. Upon graduation, Bruce took a job with ATEC Associates in Cincinnati, Ohio as a geotechnical engineer for the foundation engineering consultant firm. In 1978 after two years in Cincinnati, Bruce returned to Oklahoma City to work with his father at Atlas Paving Company.

With Bruce Smith assuming more responsibility every year at the Atlas Companies, Paul Smith decided to sell his stock to the Hugh Smith family in 1980. Bruce became the primary owner and chief officer at Atlas Paving Company and Atlas Asphalt Products, the asphalt manufacturing company. In 1983 the Smiths installed a new "state-of-the-art" drum mix asphalt plant with full recycling capabilities. The new technology included a bag house for dust control, full-computerized control system, 400-ton storage silos, and reclaimed asphalt recycling abilities. This improvement solidified the Atlas companies' place as a leader in the highly competitive paving industry, which they still maintain to this day.

In 1980 Hugh's son-in-law and husband to Hugh's youngest daughter, Connie, came to work at the family business. Richard K. Metheny had graduated from Oklahoma State University with a B.S. degree in finance in 1976. After several different jobs in the banking and finance industry, Rick came to work at Makins Concrete as a salesman and assistant to Hugh. As before, Paul Smith decided to sell his stock to the Smith family and, in 1982, all ownership of the original Makins Concrete Company was held within the Hugh Smith family.

Opposite, top: Atlas Paving Company forming a concrete roadway using Metheny Concrete, 1994.

Opposite, middle: Metheny Concrete's continuous mix concrete plant supplying concrete to Atlas Paving Company, 1994.

Opposite, bottom: A present-day Atlas Paving Company road paver.

Top, left: Richard K. Metheny, president of Metheny Concrete Products from 1987 to the present.

Top, right: Bruce L. Smith, president of Atlas Paving Company and Atlas Asphalt Products from 1987 to the present.

Below: The 2001 Christmas photo of Hugh and Melba Smith, with children and grandchildren.

Metheny advanced to assume a major role in the operation of the concrete company and became operations officer in 1985.

Hugh Smith continued to mentor and guide his successors in their development as business leaders until his retirement in 1987. Rick acquired full ownership of Makins Concrete and reorganized and renamed the company Metheny Concrete Products. Materco, the equipment holding company, remained intact.

Today the four companies–Atlas Paving Company, Atlas Asphalt Products, Metheny Concrete Products, and Materco–share a common office built by Hugh Smith in 1974 at 3800 Northwest 8th Street in Oklahoma City. Although the companies operate independently, a common bond established through the legacy of Hugh Smith forever binds the companies together. Bruce Smith and Rick Metheny, brother-in-laws, are partners in various real estate and commercial ventures, recently in retail strip shipping centers and commercial batting cages.

Hugh Smith can still be seen at the corporate offices visiting with his son and son-in-law. A lake house, traveling, OSU sporting events, and the activities of his eight grandchildren occupy his time. Hugh's accomplishments and influences in this world came as Corporate president and CEO, Board member and Director of the Asphalt and Concrete trade associations, OSU School of Civil Engineering Board member, City, County and State

Specification committee member, businessman, company founder, mentor, father, father-in-law, grandfather, Sunday school teacher, baseball coach and Christian servant. His legacy includes a son and son-in-law who have followed him in business and have maintained the attributes that made him a successful man—hard work, integrity, dedication, family loyalty, and devotion to God.

The American dream still exists in Oklahoma City.

# AMERICAN FLORAL SERVICES

American Floral Services (AFS) began in the small Oklahoma City garage apartment located behind the home of its founder, Herman Meinders. In membership numbers it grew to be the nation's largest flowers-by-wire service. Recently the company merged with Teleflora, headquartered in Los Angeles, with the AFS office in Oklahoma City as a major branch.

Meinders, a native of Minnesota, was reared on the farm of his German immigrant father. He had to forego sports and other extracurricular school activities in order to tend his farm chores. He began to learn the sales trade working for the JCPenney Company part-time while attending high school. It evolved into a full-time job following graduation, while he saved money for college.

Seeking a warmer climate for his future career, Meinders transferred with the JCPenney Company to the Mayfair store in Oklahoma City and to attend Oklahoma City University. After a year at OCU he moved to Florida, hoping to attend Florida Southern, but was unable to find a job that would help pay tuition. After working at several jobs at a supermarket in Tampa, he took a job as a salesman for the National Florists' Directory and began a life on the road, visiting florists throughout the United States. This was his entry into what would become his life's career.

He learned the wire service end of the floral industry from ground up, calling on every flower shop in 37 states and working all 50 states. During these years he became acquainted with thousands of florists nationwide, leading to a position with Florafax Delivery, Inc., where he became vice president of sales. However, when a change of ownership brought in new people and Meinders found himself demoted, he made the decision to start his own wire service, and American Floral Services was born in October 1970.

Starting with $500 capital and three employees, he put sales representatives on the road on a commission basis and the company grew. Within two years the new company had nearly three thousand members and had moved to an office across the street from his apartment.

AFS operates as a clearing-house in the floral industry. It guarantees that the order is transmitted correctly and that the florist

✧

*Herman and LaDonna Meinders.*

delivering the flowers receives payment. The guarantee goes further. The flowers must reach the destination on time and in good condition.

Through the years, Meinders brought many innovations to the floral industry, beginning with "no-charge sending," which meant that the florist sending the order to another AFS member was not charged a fee. It was not long before the larger wire services began to follow his lead on this and other new ideas, which were to come. AFS was also the first company in the nation to introduce a cash rebate, adding millions of dollars to the profits of individual flower shops.

Later Meinders began a trade magazine, *Professional Floral Designer*, which soon became the industry standard. The magazine offers practical help and advice to florists. Recognizing a need, he began to develop an educational program, which has reached thousands of florists and designers from around the world. Many have traveled to the home office in Oklahoma City to attend seminars and brush up on professional skills in everything from floral wedding designs to financial record keeping and computer technology. Participants in these seminars have come from as far away as Taiwan and Australia and as near as a few blocks away.

The company designed its financial and accounting computer software, called Rosebud, sold it to more than three thousand florists, and trained shop owners and employees to use it.

Because of the time differences around the world, the company's international department works late in the evening and on weekends to ensure that there are no disappointments for weddings, birthdays, christenings or funerals.

AFS has transmitted flower orders to Mikhail Gorbachev, former president of the Soviet Union; Queen Elizabeth and other members of the British royal family; and entertainers Michael Jackson and Julio Iglesias.

In 1982, with 15,000 subscribing members, AFS moved into a 43,000-square-foot facility in Oklahoma City, equipped to handle its huge number of orders as far away as Australia, Korea, the Netherlands, and South Africa.

Herman Meinders has supported the floral industry in countless ways on local, state and national levels. In the early 1980s he was a co-founder of the World Flower Council, which encompasses floral designers, growers, and shop owners from many countries. The Council is dedicated to promoting world peace through the beauty of the flower. He has served as chairman of the Council, which he has supported with both financial and staff support. WFC meets annually in countries throughout the world to share ideas, participate in design shows and expand its members' knowledge of the floral industry.

In 1985 Tom Butler came to AFS from Michigan, becoming president of the company, and Meinders became chairman. Meinders sold most of his interest in the company in 1994 to devote more time to his ranch in eastern Oklahoma, and to civic and community service. Within the community he serves on the board of trustees of Oklahoma City University, where he spent his only college year, and was chairman of its executive committee. The OCU business school has been named in his honor. Meinders and his wife, LaDonna, give numerous scholarships each semester to students in the Meinders School of Business.

The Meinders' contributions to the community have been many. They have included the Meinders Scout Shop at the headquarters of the Last Frontier Council of the Boy Scouts of America. Other major contributions have included The Meinders Gardens in the Myriad Gardens complex, The Joe Grandee Museum at the National Cowboy and Western Heritage Museum, the Sales and Marketing Association (SMEI) Academy of Achievement at Enterprise Square, USA, the Phillips Pavilion at the Governor's Mansion, and the coming dome for the State Capitol, to name just a few.

He has been inducted into the Oklahoma Heritage Hall of Fame, the SMEI Academy of Achievement, and the OCU Hall of Honor. He has received the Silver Beaver Award from the Boy Scouts, the Distinguished Service Award and an honorary doctorate from Oklahoma City University, the Liberty Bell Award from the Oklahoma County Bar Association, the Melvin Jones Fellow Award from Lions International Foundation, the Order of Merit and the Order of Achievement Awards from Lambda Chi Alpha national fraternity.

He currently serves as chairman of the American Floral Endowment, an organization devoted to research for new floral varieties, care and handling of flowers, and insect control without the use of pesticides.

Under Butler the company expanded its seminars and other programs serving the floral industry. In November 2000 AFS merged with Teleflora, with Butler serving as chairman and Meinders as chairman emeritus of the combined companies.

Certainly AFS and its founder have made a major impact in Oklahoma City and Oklahoma County, and from all indications, this impact will continue.

❖

*The headquarters building of American Floral Services (AFS) in Oklahoma City, now a division of Los Angeles-based Teleflora.*

# GODDARD READY MIX CONCRETE COMPANY

Walk into the headquarters building of Goddard Ready Mix Concrete Company, and you will almost feel that you have walked into an art museum. Japanese art adorns the walls, mixed with pictures of early concrete plants, family pictures, displays and sport trophies from the successful company-sponsored teams. The walls of each room—even the restrooms—are decorated with unusual and attractive designs. You hardly realize that you are entering the offices of a company dealing with outside construction.

All are the design of Neoma Eva Goddard, who helped her husband, Kenneth Eugene Goddard, to build the company from a paving company started in their home. Over the years, Goddard has provided most of the paving and concrete services in eastern Oklahoma County.

Today the company is in the second generation of the family, managed by daughter, Kelly Goddard Cooke. Kelly takes pride in having started in the business at age seven.

Kenneth, founder of the company, was reared in Choctaw during the great depression, and experienced the family joblessness that affected many households, including eviction from a home. He entered

*Right: Neoma and Kenneth Goddard at an Oklahoma Ready Mix Concrete Association function.*

*Below: Goddard Ready Mix Concrete Company was in business thirty-seven years with the first plant, purchase from Stokes Ready-Mix.*

the military service near the end of World War II, serving as an Army cryptographer until early 1950. After which he took a job with the Federal Aeronautical Administration, where he met Neoma, and was married in 1951. Later he took a position managing a TG&Y store while she worked at Tinker Air Force Base as a secretary to a senior officers.

Kenneth's father had been a plasterer, which gave him an acquaintance with mortar, if not concrete. His own experience in paving began at age 14, when he worked from dawn to dusk for 25 cents an hour. He began his own paving business in the mid-1950s, and in 1958 he moved into the ready-mix concrete business working out of his home with a three man paving crew and three wheelbarrows. His principal ready-mix plant remains in its original location behind his home on Northeast Tenth Street near Post Road in Midwest City.

Although he performs some jobs throughout Oklahoma County, the principal concentration of work is in eastern Oklahoma City, Del City, Midwest City, and Choctaw.

The company—a non-union organization—takes pride in its long-time employees. One of the members of its original crew, Louie Locke remains with the company. Kelly recalls that another member, Raymond Ballard, was working for the company at the time she was born.

Kelly is a long-time employee, particularly if you count her early years working Saturdays with sand and gravel at age seven. She was paid three cents for each shovel of sand and a nickel for each shovel of gravel. Before she was nine she was backing up the car on the property. By ten she was operating the tractor, and by twelve she could run the loading machine. By sixteen she was breaking concrete with a sledgehammer—not bad for a girl who today weighs about ninety pounds and is less than five feet tall.

Kelly is the middle child of three girls and the only one who chose the concrete business for a career. All are graduates of the University of Central Oklahoma. Her sisters, Jean Ann Southern and Susie Evelyn Dealy, received masters degrees in education and public relations, and chose careers in the teaching and adult education professions. Kelly has an administrative business degree.

The family has played an important role in the Oklahoma Ready-Mix Concrete Association. Kelly remembers attending her first association convention at Western Hills Lodge at seven. At that time her father and mother began their important role of rebuilding the association. Kenneth served multiple terms as president, and Neoma served as secretary-treasurer. Both have been accorded the honor of being named lifetime members of the association.

Most of the streets and paved lots of eastern Oklahoma County are the handiwork of the Goddard Concrete Company. They include all the streets in the Windsong Addition, the Choctaw Vo-Tech School, the concrete work at Choctaw High School, most of the development areas of W. P. "Bill" Atkinson, the Kennington Addition, Hudiburg Chevrolet, the Ridgefield Addition, and many areas of the Oklahoma City Zoo.

The company is occasionally called to do volunteer work and usually responds. An example is the concrete for the restoration of the historic round barn of Arcadia.

The business, association and his family were the principal interests of Kenneth. Kenneth and his family were active in the Nicoma Park Church of Christ. The company is active in the Midwest City and Choctaw

Chambers of Commerce, the Oklahoma and National Home Builders' Associations, and the Oklahoma Safety Council, among other organizations. Kenneth has been honored nationally by being listed in the book, *Who's Who Among Executives and Professionals*.

Health problems plagued Kenneth in the late 1980s and he closed the paving division of the company in 1989. By the mid-1990s, realizing the extent of his health problems, he semi-retired, and named Kelly as president of the company. He died in August 1997.

Kelly, in addition to being the first woman in Oklahoma to be a Certified Concrete Technician, has received many honors. She is a certified miner with the State of Oklahoma, listed in *Who's Who Among Young Woman in America* and has been an actress working with the Whodunit Dining Room Mystery Theater in Oklahoma City. She has been active among "Clowns for Christ" and is known as Butterbrain. At the Nicoma Park Church of Christ, she teaches the Children's Bible Study hour during Sunday church services.

What about the future? Certainly there will always be construction and the need for concrete in building and paving and Goddard Concrete Company, under its second generation of leadership is excited about continuing to play an active and important role in the community.

❖

*Goddard Ready Mix Concrete Company plant at 10100 Northeast Tenth Street in Midwest City, May 2000.*

# THE NAIFEH FAMILY

In the early years after the turn of the century, the nation of Lebanon, in Asia Minor, was part of the Ottoman Empire. It was a strictly Moslem empire, and in 1910 young men were being conscripted into a Moslem Army.

This type of conscription didn't set well with Zeak Naifeh and his family, because the Naifehs were Christians and opposed fighting with a Moslem force. Two of his brothers had already emigrated to the United States and wanted fourteen-year-old Zeak to join them.

However, getting to the United States would not be easy for Zeak. There was no money for such a trip, and he would have to earn his fare before leaving Lebanon.

The first lap of his journey ended in Marsailles, France, where he worked on the docks to earn enough money to pay his fare to the United States. Finally, having earned the money, he traveled by ship to New York, going to Ellis Island to complete his immigration papers.

He was able to communicate only in Arabic, but friends met him at Ellis Island and put him on a train. They gave him a sign telling the conductor to put him off at Sapulpa, Oklahoma. There, at age fourteen, Zeak went to work for his brothers, who were in the food retail business. While on the job,

and in his spare time, he began to learn the English language on his own.

By the time he was twenty years old he was ready to go into his own business. He moved to Bristow, where he opened his own wholesale grocery. It was in Bristow where Zeak met and married Rose Homsey. Together they had four children, Selma, Robert, Leileh, and Franklin.

In 1930 Zeak sold his business in Bristow to fulfill his dream of making a trip back to Lebanon. At that time, Lebanon was no longer a part of the Ottoman Empire, but was a French mandate. Zeak's intention was to make it only a long vacation, but due to the depression in the United States, he was advised by his brothers to remain in Lebanon.

By 1935 the young family returned to Oklahoma City, where Zeak opened Market Wholesale, a wholesale grocery company, with partners. Market Wholesale was located among the wholesale produce houses west of the public market. Two years later this store closed and Zeak opened Sooner Sales Company, dealing wholesale with candy and tobacco. This company was located at 330 West Grand, south of the streetcar Interurban Terminal Building. It remained there one year, then moved to 221 West Reno, in an area that is now a part of the Myriad Gardens. The

company remained there throughout the World War II period, then moved to 1009 West Reno where he built his own building.

In 1959, shortly after repeal of prohibition in Oklahoma, Naifeh closed Sooner Sales Company and opened Central Liquor Company, another wholesale company. By 1966 the company had grown to such an extent that he built another building at 1009 Southwest Fourth Street. Business continued growing, and twelve years later he moved to 4001 Northwest Third Street, and currently located at Northwest Sixth and Tulsa Avenue.

Zeak Naifeh was a community supporter throughout his business career, with a particular concern for the handicapped. He was a strong supporter of St. Jude Hospital for Crippled Children in Memphis, made famous by Danny Thomas. In Oklahoma City Zeak was a leader and major supporter of St. Elijah Orthodox Church, serving as its treasurer and as the chairman of its board. He played a

major role in raising the money, which built the church building at Northwest Sixteenth and Pennsylvania.

Never forgetting his Lebanese roots, he sent money back to the village where he was born and reared to bring electricity to the community. Mrs. Naifeh was equally involved in church work.

Naifeh died in 1987 at the age of ninety-one, and his wife died in 1992.

Partners in the Central Liquor Company today are Robert Z. and Franklin K. Naifeh, sons of the founder. Equally involved in the community as their parents, the brothers helped to sponsor the cancer center at St. Anthony Hospital in memory of their sister, Selma, who died in 1997. They also contributed to the Wellness Center at Oklahoma City University in memory of their mother and father and helped to build the St. Elijah Antiochian Orthodox Christian Church at Northwest 150th and May Avenue.

✧

*This building on the southwest corner of Main and Western was the location of the early wholesale grocery business of Zeak Naifeh.*

# BISHOP PAVING COMPANY AND MEGA SUPPLY CORPORATION

Sometimes it is almost by accident, or at least by chance, that one moves into a new business career unrelated to any of past experience.

This was the case of Royce Bishop, who already was highly successful as a manager in an automobile sales career when he switched gears. He resigned to purchase a machine for repairing breaks in paving, and to form a business in which he had no previous experience. Initially, it was a one-man operation. The idea came when he was observing the number of potholes in Oklahoma City streets.

"Are you crazy?" is the only comments he could get from friends and neighbors who knew of his automotive success.

That was in 1974. Today Royce's organization, Bishop Paving Company, located at 927 Southwest Sixth Street, employs nearly forty people and performs paving projects throughout Oklahoma.

Royce Bishop is the youngest of six children. Born in Garvin County and reared in Oklahoma City, graduating from Capitol Hill High School.

Drafted into the Army after graduation, he served in Korea with the Seventy-sixth Anti-Aircraft Artillery Battalion. Upon separation from the military he enrolled as a student at the University of Oklahoma combining his educational years with work in a used car lot operated by his brothers.

Royce met and married Liz Martin, an Oklahoma runner-up in the Miss Universe competition, two months after meeting her while dining out one evening.

His career blossomed and eventually was offered the United States sales manager position for the Nissan Company, maker of Datsun. This required a move to Los Angeles, California. Promising Liz the family would return within one year if she did not like California. Actually, they remained there two and one-half years, but a return visit to Oklahoma City in 1971 convinced both that this was the place to live and raise the family.

Upon learning of his impeding return, he was offered the general sales manager's position in the dealership of Fred Jones Ford. Intrigued with the challenge of moving the facility into a profit margin, he accepted, and found himself working almost around the clock to meet the challenge. Within three years sales had multiplied and he had met his goals. The arduous hours had sapped his enthusiasm. At this point he felt ready for a change and a new challenge.

This was when he began to notice potholes in streets. He inquired about it among city officials, learning the equipment and personnel was available but not the money until the next budget year to buy the asphalt needed. Learning about the machine used to lay the asphalt, he wrote the manufacturer in Waco, who invited

✧

*Above: Royce and Liz Bishop.*

*Below: Royce and Patrick Bishop, March 1995.*

him for a visit. To everyone's surprise, he bought one of the spreaders, resigned his job, and began repairing cracks and holes in lots, streets, and wherever he could get a contract. Operated the machine with the assistance of a part-time student helper and his twelve-year old son, he soon "graduated" into a variety of paving jobs, including both asphalt and concrete.

Royce learned as he went along with the help from his brother-in-law, Charles Lampkin. Lampkin, a civil engineer, had worked for H. E. Bailey in the paving area advising as he moved into various new areas of paving. Before long the company was paving and repairing streets, and pouring lots and foundation pads for stores and shopping centers.

Among their projects over the years have been paving and foundation pads for Quail Springs Mall, Silver Springs Crossing, the Sprint Building, Walgreen's, Wal-Mart and Sam's, Home Depots, Albertson's, Yukon's Integris Hospital, the new Kohl's Department Stores, Staples stores, the Baptist Hospital running track and parking lot, and the new football field at Putnam City High School, designed to be covered with Astroturf.

Another company, acquired by Royce Bishop, is Mega Supply Corporation. Mega Supply is a multi-state distributor for containers, and is also operated by a member of the extended family. The company distributes disposable plates, Styrofoam cups, trays, and other items used by supermarkets, restaurants, clubs, institutions, and other organizations in Oklahoma, Texas and Arkansas. Royce and his son-in-law, Ray Becerra,

purchased the failing Oklahoma division in 1993 renaming it, Mega Supply Corporation and moved its headquarters from Reno and Ann Arbor to 908 Southwest Fifth Street.

Ray serves as president of Mega Supply Corporation and Royce's and Liz' daughter, Sheral Becerra, is vice president and secretary-treasurer. Upon taking over the company, its annual gross sales increased from less then $2 million to $12 million.

Ray and Sheral have an eleven-year-old daughter, Nina.

Active in civic and community affairs, Royce and Liz are members of All Souls Episcopal Church. Royce is past president of the Oklahoma City Jaycees, a charter member and past president of the Capitol Hill Sertoma Club. He helped to found the Surrey Hills Lions Club, served as president, and is an active member of the Masonic body, the Shrine and the Jesters. He served two terms as president of the Capitol Hill Athletic Association and is a director of the Bank of Nichols Hills. The Jaycees named him Outstanding Young Man of Oklahoma City for the year 1965.

Son Patrick has twenty-six years experience in the paving business and served as company president for eight years. Pat and his wife, Anita, live on a farm west of Yukon, where he raises Angus cattle. His children, sixteen-year-old Jason, and 14-year-old Jessica, are active in the Yukon FFA. Both have show pigs and Jason also raises show steers. Patrick also flies his own airplane and Anita is employed by the Yukon Board of Education.

✧

*Ray Becerra, president and Sheral Bishop Becerra, vice president and secretary-treasurer of Mega Supply Corp.*

# St. Anthony Hospital

The site of the Alfred E. Murrah Building will be remembered in history for many generations as the location of one of the largest acts of domestic terrorism in American history.

However the earliest development of this site also played a major–and in this case, a positive—role in the history and heritage of Oklahoma County. It marked the beginning of the first major hospital in the county—a hospital that celebrated its one-hundredth anniversary in 1998.

One would hardly recognize the imposing St. Anthony Hospital at Northwest Tenth and Dewey in Oklahoma City as being the same institution that began in a two-story frame building with a capacity of twelve patients, opening August 1, 1898, at 219 Northwest Fourth Street.

It all began when two sisters of the St. Francis from Missouri visited this bustling frontier town soliciting contributions for St. Joseph's Hospital in Maryville. They met first with Father D. I. Lanslots, pastor of Oklahoma City's St. Joseph's Church. Lanslots responded by asking that the order establish a hospital in Oklahoma City.

A study by Mother M. Augustine Giesen, the first Superior General of the Sisters of St. Francis, along with other sisters, determined that Oklahoma City did need help.

Two months later four sisters returned to Oklahoma City and rented two wooden houses. One of these was to become the twelve-bed hospital, and the adjacent building became quarters for the sisters.

The first patient was a Jewish traveling agent from Cincinnati, treated for malarial fever. Six of the first ten patients worked for the Santa Fe Railroad and were treated for poison oak and malarial fever.

Drs. J. A. Ryan and Joseph B. Rolator treated the men. Serious operations were performed in the small hospital and the doctors succeeded with practically all their patients.

Winter brought major problems for the hospital. There was neither gas nor electricity to heat and light the rooms. Coal stoves in small rooms made cleanliness and fresh air practically impossible. The sisters were continuously on the move from one building to the other, day and night, in blizzards and bone-chilling cold. Finally, in late November, the hospital had to close. Sixty-nine patients had been cared for—twenty-eight from the Santa Fe Railroad.

*St. Anthony Hospital one hundred years ago.*

However, with the constant growth of the city, the need for a permanent hospital was increasing. To meet this need Lanslots, along with St. Anthony physicians and sisters, approached the mayor and city commission, requesting money to construct a hospital worthy of the growing city. Lanslots explained that there was not a house in town fit for surgical work. The city fathers came to the conclusion that a hospital was an urgent need and would be a blessing to the citizens. The city commissioners decided to contribute $800 to begin the campaign for funds. At that time the north and west city limits of the town were Seventh and Walker, just as it had been at the time of the Run. Frank Gault had recently platted his farm, immediately north of the city limits, into city blocks, and the block north and west of Ninth and Dewey, formerly a cornfield, was sold to St. Anthony Hospital for $600, taken from the city allotment. The remaining $200 went into the building fund.

The campaign to build the hospital began. Citizens of all creeds contributed. Some gave money. Others gave of their time or mule teams to excavate the basement or haul materials.

Eventually the money was raised and a building contract for $11,200 was let to Kennedy O'Keefe, Oklahoma City contractor, in February 1899. The cornerstone, which can still be seen at the entrance to the St. Anthony Chapel, was laid in June.

By the close of November the twenty-five-bed hospital was completed and dedicated to St. Anthony by the Vicar Apostolic of Oklahoma and Indian Territories, Right Reverend Theophile Meerschaert, and Sister Katherine Kurz was named the first sister superior.

The new hospital was a vast improvement over the frame building on Northwest Fourth Street, but it was beset with problems. It was away from the city limits and no water supply was available at the site. For more than four years, and until a 1,340-foot well was drilled near Tenth and Dewey, water was hauled in barrels and buckets from Emerson School, three blocks to its south. There was no sewer, and the Sisters reported that one Christmas was spent battling an overflowing cesspool.

There were no electric lights or power until 1902, and no natural gas until 1904. The first telephone came in 1900. Streetcars, which began in the city in 1903, reached the hospital area in 1909. The first motor ambulance was purchased in 1911.

However, despite the slowness in obtaining facilities, Oklahoma City was growing, and there was need for additional beds. The first addition came in 1905, bringing capacity to one hundred beds. Another significant addition was made in 1908, when the state's first school of nursing was established at St. Anthony.

Meanwhile, the first four-year medical and dental schools in Oklahoma Territory were established in 1905, not by the University of Oklahoma, but by Epworth University, a Methodist college that had been organized in Oklahoma City three years earlier. St. Anthony, along with the newly opened Rolater Hospital, founded by Dr. Joseph B. Rolater, became a training center for future doctors. The Epworth medical school was turned over to the University of Oklahoma in 1908. St. Anthony Hospital remains today as a key element in the training of physicians, nurses, and paramedical specialists.

The hospital's location was eulogized in St. Anthony's 1906 annual report as "perfect for hospital purposes, being removed about one-half mile from the business district."

The year 1908 brought the first x-ray to St. Anthony, only thirteen years after its invention.

St. Anthony has continued this tradition of leadership in Oklahoma with many firsts: a hospital-based pharmacy in 1925, an intensive care unit in 1963, a radioactive isotope laboratory in 1965, a mobile coronary care unit in 1969, an argon optical laser beam in 1971, a kidney transplantation in 1971, a neurological surgery institute and dialysis unit in 1972, an alcohol treatment unit in 1975, a "wellness" program in 1979, a drug-screening service for businesses in 1986, a craniofacial surgical team in 1989, and a non-teaching hospital offering accredited family practice residency in 1991. In 1995 the hospital's MRI was judged as the world's best.

Beyond its primary role as a healthcare provider, St. Anthony is a leader in renewing the heart of Oklahoma City which has suffered from the effects of the oil "bust" of the 1980s, stalled urban renewal efforts, and later the bombing of the Murrah Federal Building. The hospital takes an active leadership role in numerous community organizations.

St. Anthony offers a variety of free health education and health screenings to the community each year, as well as seminars on nutrition, stroke awareness, parenting, and substance abuse prevention. It is also the second largest provider of care to the indigent in the community.

The hospital has grown tremendously from the twelve-bed facility but it has never forgotten that its mission is to serve people.

✧

*Above: The front entrance of St. Anthony Hospital.*

*Below: Among the many sophisticated instruments at St. Anthony Hospital is this linear accelerator, used in the treatment of brain cancer.*

# MCCONNELL CONSTRUCTION, INC.

❖

*Left: John McConnell, Sr.*

*Right: John McConnell, Jr.*
COURTESY OF TAYLOR MADE PHOTOGRAPHY.

Unlike a period three to four generations ago, which many Oklahomans continue to remember well, we have learned to take for granted the smoothness of today's highways, as well as the secondary and "farm to market" roads. The principal complaint with highways today is when re-surfacing becomes necessary; we lose patience with the repair vehicles that may impair traffic.

What we often fail to appreciate is the effort made, sometimes around the clock, to keep our Oklahoma roads in the condition we always expect to find them.

A good example of those who keep Oklahoma roads in good traveling shape is the McConnell Construction, Inc., which specializes in asphalt surfacing of roads and supplies asphalt to other paving companies.

President and chief executive officer of the company is John McConnell, Jr., who took over and has greatly expanded a paving company created by his father in 1944.

McConnell Construction is headquartered in far west Oklahoma County, at 8251 West Reno. However, the company and its equipment are more visible along any road needing to be paved or repaired in Oklahoma County.

Although McConnell Construction deals in asphalt paving and sales today, it first grew as a concrete paving company in the early 1960s, when John McConnell, Sr. joined with a partner in the founding of the Brooks-

McConnell Construction, Inc. At that time, the company paved a large span of Interstate 35 through all of Logan County and was involved in five paving jobs at the same time, installing more steel than can be found in the giant San Francisco Golden Gate Bridge.

His son, John McConnell, Jr., originally had other career ideas. He attended Oklahoma A&M, with agriculture as his goal. His degree was in animal husbandry, with minors in geology, organic chemistry, and agricultural engineering.

However, while attending college, he participated in the Air Force ROTC program, and was selected as the outstanding ROTC student at Oklahoma A&M for 1956. He graduated with a second lieutenant's commission and an active duty military requirement. This resulted in service with the United States Air Force between 1956 and 1959.

By the time he was separated from the service, he had switched his career goals from agriculture to paving, and joined his father in the company, working in every job capacity until he followed his father as president.

Back when the younger McConnell first joined the company, he was not satisfied with retaining the company strictly for concrete paving. Within a few years after he entered the company, he changed the emphasis of his effort to asphalt paving. He first entered the asphalt business in 1964, and one year later he purchased the company's first portable hot mix asphalt plant. As time progressed, the paving operation became exclusively in asphalt. As a paver in asphalt, the McConnell firm soon became one of the top paving companies in the state and was recognized nationwide. One year they ranked 14th in the nation in output. McConnell Construction introduced the first silo for hot asphalt storage in the state and also brought the first vibrating roller for hot mix asphalt compaction in the state.

Conservation is another area in which McConnell Construction has played a leading role. The company established the first asphalt plant for recycling asphalt in Oklahoma.

Asphalt, which is a product of rock, sand and oil, never wears out, but eventually the surface becomes beaten by traffic and requires repair and replacement. Since it does not wear out, this provides the opportunity of conservation through recycling, and recycling of asphalt is an effort of McConnell Construction, Inc. Most of the asphalt produced and used by the company is twenty-five percent recycled.

McConnell also performed the first project of the Oklahoma Department of Transportation with petromat under the overlaid hot mix asphalt and the first company in the state using insoluble rock in the surface course.

Twice the company was runner-up for the Sheldon G. Hayes Award from the National Asphalt Pavement Association—first in 1972 for paving on State Highway 62 west of Lawton, and later, in 1976, for paving on State Highway 112 in LeFlore County.

In the concrete area they received the National Award for Excellence from the American Concrete Pavement Association in 1997 for the paving of Southwest Fifteenth Street between Portland and Meridian.

Both the father and son have played leadership roles in the state and national associations in the construction industry. John, Sr. was a past president of the Oklahoma Association of General Contractors and served on the board of Oklahoma Associated General Contractors and was active in the Masonic bodies. John, Jr. was the first president of the

Oklahoma Asphalt Pavement Association, and served on the board of the Association of General Contractors and the Oklahoma Municipal Contractors Association.

John and his wife Margaret have between them two sons and two daughters. John's daughter, Kimberly Kay, is a nurse in Tulsa. His son John "Jay" is in investments. Brent McKee and his wife are in the interior design business in Los Angeles. Leslie Williams is a housewife in Oklahoma City.

✧

*This McConnell Construction Inc. plant at 8301 Northwest First Street is designed to produce hot mix asphalt for paving.*

# OKLAHOMA MEDICAL RESEARCH FOUNDATION

✧

*Above: Sir Alexander Fleming, renowned British scientist and discoverer of Penicillin, dedicated OMRF in 1949.*

*Below: OMRF's main building, which was renamed the Chapman Research Building and Pavilion in 2000, was OMRF's first structure. The significant remodeling and renovation was designed by Miles Associates, an Oklahoma City-based architecture and design firm.*

When a small group of graduates from the University of Oklahoma College of Medicine began a campaign following the close of World War II to develop a medical research facility, they couldn't have foreseen that it would grow into the Oklahoma Medical Research Foundation of today.

Today, more than fifty-five years later, the dream they envisioned is at its original location at 825 Northeast Thirteenth Street employs nearly five hundred people, and is anticipating construction of a six-story research tower.

OMRF is recognized as one of the top medical research institutes in the nation. OMRF is a private, independent facility, receiving no direct governmental appropriation, operating on contributions, competitive research grants, and memorials. Their memorial program is a major source of income, bringing about $650,000 each year. OMRF is a direct recipient of the Chapman Trusts, which support salaries and operational expenses. Every dollar contributed to OMRF through gifts and memorials goes exclusively to research in Oklahoma.

The Foundation is fundamentally separate from the university; however, the two organizations collaborate in many ways. In 2000 they were awarded a $22-million grant from the National Institutes of Health to study immunology and molecular biology.

In 1946 OMRF was chartered as a charitable, nonprofit research and training organization for medical science, its chartered purpose is "promoting the improvement of human health and well-being." During the next two years, more than $2.35 million was raised for construction and operational support. The Oklahoma Legislature deeded a plot of land directly east of the medical school to be used as a building site, and a forty-one-member board of directors was formed to assume administrative responsibility.

This board authorized construction of the main structure as a laboratory research building and dedication ceremonies featured Sir Alexander Fleming, the British scientist and Nobel Prize winner who discovered penicillin. By mid-1950 the first forty laboratories were ready for use, and plans were underway for additional construction.

Two years later, a sixteen-bed hospital ward was completed for clinical studies. Grants from the National Institutes of Health were supplemented by individual contributions from throughout the state.

In 1956 the Fleming Scholar program was implemented, beginning one of the most successful scientific outreach programs aimed at senior high school and college students. Open only to Oklahomans, the Fleming Scholar program has marked the beginning of many a distinguished career.

In 1959 the Foundation made international history when lab assistant Jordan Tang discovered gastricsin, the second enzyme ever identified in human gastric juice.

The Foundation received a big boost when J. A. and Leta Chapman established trusts. The couple began support in 1949, but the second Chapman Trust provided financial stability that was not previously present.

In 1970 Dr. Colin McLeod, who gained national recognition for his role in the discovery of DNA, became the Foundation's first full-time, salaried president.

The graduate education program was established in 1971 to help develop talent in a wide variety of research areas and to train physician-scientists. Today the program has been re-established with the University of Oklahoma as the Presbyterian Health Foundation M.D./Ph.D. Program.

Dr. Reagan Bradford in 1971 was appointed head of the Cardiovascular Research Program, which had its major thrust in chemotherapy in several types of cancer.

The Foundation constructed a freestanding office building, the Rogers Building, named for the Foundation's long-time friend and benefactor, John Rogers of Tulsa.

In 1972 scientists and physicians worldwide adopted the lipoprotein classification and naming system developed by Dr. Petar Alaupovic, head of the Lipid and Lipoprotein Laboratory. In 1979 the Omar B. Milligan Research Library was opened and dedicated. Later it was enlarged, adding electron microscopy suites and the Darlene Milligan Plaza.

In 1981 Dr. Morris Reichlin was named head of the Foundation's new Arthritis and Immunology Research Program. Reichlin developed "The Reichlin Profile," the definitive diagnostic test for lupus.

In 1982 the Cardiovascular Research Program turned to the study of heart attacks on the cellular level, studying the chemical changes that take place in the heart during and after an attack. Dr. Charles Esmon, now head of the Cardiovascular Biology Research Program, was named Oklahoma's first Howard Hughes Medical Institute Investigator and was the first named outside a university setting. The Ed F. Massman Cancer Research Building was built in 1988, housing the Molecular and Cell Biology Research Program. The Foundation Scholar Program for high school science teachers was established that year. The William H. Bell Building, named for the Tulsa attorney and longtime board member, was dedicated, housing administrative offices and research laboratories.

Dr. Robert Floyd discovered a compound called PBN reversed brain aging in gerbils, and Dr. Jordan Tang developed a gene that stops the growth of the AIDS virus in culture.

In 1995 a test for measuring a blood factor, which may be present in people at high risk for heart disease, was developed by Dr. James Morrissey. Drs. Ron and Joan Conaway discovered a key element in understanding of the von Hippel-Lindau (VHL) suppressor gene, whose loss of function results in predisposition to cancer, particularly kidney cancer. The NIH Lupus Multiplex Registry and Repository was established at the Foundation in 1995 through a $5-million contract from the National Institutes of Health.

In 1998 Drs. Judith James and John Harley, head of the Arthritis and Immunology, discovered a significant association between the Epstein-Barr virus and lupus, raising the suspicion that EBV might be a culprit in the development of the disease.

Also that year, Drs. Jordan Tang and Cai Zhang detailed a three-dimensional structure of the blood clotting factor, plasminogen, which may help devise new ways to provide drugs to dissolve blood clots, such as those in a heart attack or stroke.

Early in 2000, OMRF's Protein Studies team, led by Tang, identified the enzyme "memapsin 2," which scientists believe is one of the enzymes directly responsible for Alzheimer's disease. Most important, the team was able to develop an inhibitor to stop the enzyme and create a "blueprint" of the structure. These developments will assist in the creation and design of new drugs to treat Alzheimer's.

The Foundation and its scientists have received many national awards. One significant award was the gold medal of the American Aging Association, presented to Dr. Robert Floyd for his accomplishments in the field of aging research. Dr. Judith James received the Presidential Early Career Award from President Clinton, comparable to the Nobel Prize for young investigators. James is an Oklahoman and the first rheumatologist to receive this distinction. Dr. Tang received the Pioneer Award, a one million dollar research grant, from the National Alzheimer's Association in 2001.

Expansion continues into the new millennium. In the year 2000 the Foundation received a $5-million grant from the Donald W. Reynolds Foundation for construction of a genetics center. This center will be constructed as a new floor atop the current William H. Bell Building.

And what about tomorrow? Whatever tomorrow holds, the OMRF, its board and scientists will continue to make important scientific contributions: from understanding the basic functions of life to the treatment of diseases that have long plagued mankind. OMRF continues to pursue its mission …*that more may live longer, healthier lives.*

❖

*Above: Jordan Tang, Ph.D., began his research career at OMRF in 1959. As a graduate student, he discovered gastricsin, the second gastric enzyme to be identified. His work with acid proteases has yielded significant findings in AIDS and Alzheimer's research. Today, he holds the J. G. Puterbaugh Chair in Medical Research and serves as Head of the Protein Studies program.*

*Below: At OMRF, Charles Esmon, Ph.D., has gained national recognition for his work in cardiovascular disease. Dr. Esmon, Head of the Cardiovascular Biology research program and Lloyd Noble Chair in Cardiovascular Research, was the first Oklahoman to be named a Howard Hughes Medical Institute Investigator. He was also the first researcher to be named a Hughes Investigator outside a university setting.*

# CRESCENT MARKET

When you enter the doors of Crescent Market, at 6409 Avondale Drive in Nichols Hills Plaza, you immediately recognize that you are in a completely different kind of store.

There has to be something unique about this establishment to survive, grow, and prosper in a three-generation period in which virtually every grocery in the nation has been absorbed into chains. However, the uniqueness is immediately noticeable.

Instead of tile, you will find red carpeting covering every aisle in the shopping area. Go to the meat section and you will not find packaged meat. Instead there will be a team of butchers cutting the meat you select to please your desire. The selection goes far beyond the traditional packaged beef, pork and chicken found in most chain stores. Instead there will be a wide selection, such as ostrich, buffalo, smoked oysters, and domestic and imported caviar.

If it is not your first trip to the Crescent Market, you are likely to be greeted by your own name as you enter the store. If shopping gets tiresome, you will find a comfortable, hand-carved eighteenth century couch for relaxing and enjoying a cup of complimentary coffee and a cookie. In the wintertime there will be a large fireplace facing you with logs a-burning.

Is this some new kind of store? Actually it is not. It is the oldest store in Oklahoma County, established almost immediately following the Run of 1889. Naturally, the store has gone through changes over the years, advancing from a small frame hut with a storage lean-to in its front, to the best-of-its-kind store fronts on the Main Street of a growing city, to the choice location in the city's first then-residential area shopping center, to its present location in the shopping area of what is considered by many to be the most prestigious residential area in the county.

It all began when twenty-one-year-old John L. Wyatt joined a five-wagon caravan that trekked southwesterly to Wellington, Kansas. He then went to Arkansas City, from where he boarded the Santa Fe train for Oklahoma City. There he opened a grocery store, constructing an 18-by-24-foot frame building with a sleeping area in the rear of the store. The store carried his name at that time.

It was in 1906, when John D. Thomas and John Lloyd bought the store, and changed the name to Crescent Grocery and Market. However, the location and the dedication to customer service remained the same. As years passed, there were new owners, enlargement to the existing building and two moves to larger locations, but throughout this period, all locations were on Main Street, near the center of the business district. Even during this early period, the store had a reputation for offering fancy and exotic imported foods and providing a delivery service whenever requested. Early deliveries were by horse and wagon.

By 1927 Oklahoma City was expanding,

❖

*Above: Crescent Market of the 1920s located at 323 West Main Street.*

*Below: An aisle of fruits and vegetables at the present Crescent Market at 6409 Avondale Drive in Nichols Hills Plaza.*

downtown parking was becoming difficult, and choice homes of the city were located between Northwest Tenth and Northwest Twenty-third Street. It was then that Thomas decided to construct the city's first residential area shopping center, at Northwest Tenth and Walker. This was also the streetcar junction between the Walker line from downtown and the Classen Boulevard line. Thomas called this first away-from-downtown shopping Center Plaza Court, and he made Crescent Market the anchor store. There it remained until 1963.

It was in 1942, shortly after the beginning of World War II, that J. L. Cole and Art L. Pemberton acquired the store. This began a 60 year, and three-generation ownership and management of Crescent Market under the same family. Shortly after the war Cole left the firm, and in 1951 Art E. Pemberton joined his father in the business. Later the younger Art Pemberton succeeded his father as its president and manager.

In 1963, realizing that a large segment of its customers had moved farther northwest, the Pembertons relocated the Crescent Market to a twenty-thousand-square-foot building in Nichols Hills Plaza, near Northwest Sixty-third and Western. Home deliveries were discontinued in 1975, but the personal service of the market continues.

The reputation of the Crescent Market for quality has been legend since its opening in 1889, but its highest reputation has been in its produce and meat departments. With eight full-time butchers, who cut meat to the customers' specifications, the meat department produces thirty percent of the market's annual sales.

The produce department operates a special ripening room with controlled humidity and temperature and makes up twelve percent of total sales. Fresh fruits and vegetables are brought in from the West Coast when they are not available on the local market, and out-of-season fruits are air shipped from South America.

Today the Crescent Market operates under the leadership of its third generation manager and president, Robert A. Pemberton, with his father, Art E. Pemberton serving as a consultant.

What about the future? Who knows? But Robert's daughter, Alexis, in a first grade assignment a few years ago, indicated that she wanted to run the Crescent Market when she grows up.

Of one thing we can be confident. The reputation for quality, which has covered more than 110 years, is in good hands and we can expect it to continue.

❖

*Four generations of Pembertons (from left to right): Art L. Pemberton, Art E. Pemberton, Robert A. Pemberton, and Alexis Pemberton.*

# KIMRAY, INC.

Founded in the late summer of 1948, Kimray, Inc. provides service to clients in the petroleum industry and medical profession throughout the world.

Entrepreneur Garman Kimmell, founder and president of the company, is a unique combination of personalities. Kimmell moved from a secure position as a research engineer with a prospering company to invest all his earnings in a new company, based upon an idea he was convinced would work. He is an inventor—a "night person"—who spends afternoons and nights in a laboratory adjacent to his backyard garage, creating ideas for new products. Kimmell has more than twenty-five patents to his credit and is involved in the community, in both cultural and patriotic activities, and has been recognized for his generous contributions.

Kimmell was born in Maryland and moved to Bartlesville when he was an infant and later moved to Wichita, Kansas, where his father was involved in the oil business. Kimmell attended Wichita State University and the University of Oklahoma, where he earned a master of science degree in petroleum engineering.

While at OU, and after graduation, he was employed as a research engineer at Black Sivalls & Bryson. BS&B constructed oil and gas separators, tanks, and gas pipeline equipment. Kimmell received his first nine patents while working for BS&B.

When BS&B was purchased in 1947, Kimmell was faced with a possible required move to Kansas City. With the undesirable choice of a move or the challenge of starting his own company to develop and market products that he would create, he chose the latter. Gwynn Raymond, a fellow BS&B engineer, and Kimmell formed their own company in an abandoned grocery store at 215 South Western, in the town of Britton, north of Oklahoma City.

One of their early projects was Kimmell's stabilization of a valve for the petroleum industry that had been created in Houston, Texas. The valve was successful in the petroleum industry, and soon the company was farming castings out to two foundries in order to meet the demand. During this period, Kimmell, with the investment of his father, purchased Raymond's holdings in the company.

By 1951 the company had outgrown its building in Britton (by then a part of Oklahoma City) and purchased a ten-thousand-square-foot structure at 52 Northwest Forty-second Street from the Oklahoma Industries Authority, which was developing the Santa Fe Industrial District. Kimray was the fourth company to move into the new development behind TG&Y, Macklanburg-Duncan, and King's Juices. Kimray produced a gas dehydration device that Kimmell had first conceived while visiting with a professor friend at the University of Oklahoma.

Next came computers. Kimray bought into a computer company and formed a fully owned subsidiary, Computer Institute of Oklahoma. Briefly, until Kimray sold the company, it was manufacturing and marketing computers of the 1960s styles.

The company entered the medical field almost by accident. Kimmell, whose creative ability had been recognized by professionals in various fields, was asked by a surgery team in 1957 to develop a temperature-lowering device that could be used in open-heart surgery. Not necessarily expecting it to become a commercial item, Kimmell worked on the project in his home laboratory at night. When it was completed, he was asked to be a part of the operating team and found himself

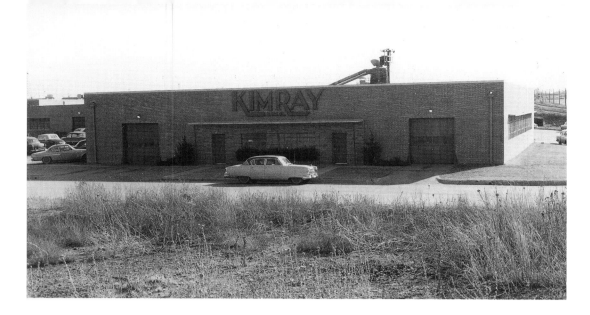

in physician's garb, assisting by operating the heart-lung machine that he had created.

Kimray Medical Associates was formed to build this device, and a surfactometer, which measures changes in the surface tension of biological fluids. Kimmell also invented the Greenfield Vena Cava filter, which is placed in the vein to catch blood clots produced in the lower extremities.

Kimray, along with other companies serving the petroleum industry, experienced a downturn when the oil boom of the middle 1980s ended. While other companies across the nation were laying off workers, Kimray kept its employees on the payroll. For 18 months, more than 90 employees were assigned to public service for charitable and nonprofit agencies, as well as the city and state, while being paid by Kimray. This action attracted attention throughout the nation.

The company also became involved in the Institute in Basic Life Principles, an outreach organization for troubled youths and their families. Its program includes job training and motivation efforts in a spiritual setting. Kimray purchased the ten-story former Holiday Inn on Main Street and donated it to the Institute for training purposes.

Meanwhile, son-in-law and executive vice president of Kimray, Tom Hill, became involved with the Institute, serving on its board of directors. Hill is the founder of Character First, providing character training on the job, in the classroom, and at home.

Beginning in Oklahoma City, this organization now has spread throughout the world, and Hill has spoken for Character First in many nations, including Mexico, New Zealand, Japan, China, and Taiwan.

Beyond his company activities, Kimmell is involved in cultural activities, particularly the Oklahoma City Philharmonic Orchestra. He has recorded concerts for more than thirty years, and for this and other contributions, he has received the Governor's Arts Award.

Kimmell has a strong commitment to patriotism and free enterprise, and for many years he served as chairman of the annual Oklahoma City Independence Day Parade. For his patriotic activity, he has been honored with the Individual Service Award of Freedoms Foundation at Valley Forge.

For his lasting contributions to his community, the Oklahoma City/County Historical Society recognized him in 1999 as a "Pathmaker of Oklahoma County," an honor for lifetime contributions accorded annually by the society to not more than four individuals.

✧

*Above: An early photograph of Kimray, Inc.*

*Below: Kimray, which conceived and organized Character First, sponsors billboards such as this with messages promoting the aims of the organization.*

## HARRY MORTGAGE COMPANY

In today's era of acquisitions and mergers in the wholesale, retail, and service business, it is difficult to find a company in the mortgage business that is strictly local and not a subsidiary of a parent bank, insurance company, or other financial institution.

Fifty years ago there were thirty or more mortgage companies in Oklahoma and Tulsa Counties. Today you can count the total number in both counties on the fingers of one hand.

An exception in Oklahoma City is Harry Mortgage Company, a four-generation institution, which at the beginning of the new century, built a beautiful new ten-thousand-square-foot facility located at 3048 North Grand Boulevard east of Will Rogers Park on a spot formerly occupied by the Christopher's Restaurant at Northwest Thirtieth and Grand Boulevard.

Harry Mortgage Company deals with both residential and commercial mortgages, but has most of its business in residential property, was organized by a father and sons team, V. M. Harry, Sr., and Robert and "Bud" Harry.

The older Harry, now deceased, was a native of Missouri, who moved to Ralston, in Pawnee County, then in Indian Territory, in 1904. There, with exception of the World War period, when he served in the Army, he was employed by the federal government—first the Home Owners Loan Corporation, and later the Federal Housing Administration.

His eldest son, Robert, now board chairman of the company, was reared in Ralston and attended Oklahoma A&M. He later received a law degree from the University of Oklahoma.

His education, like his father's banking career, was split by war. Robert was commissioned through the ROTC program at Oklahoma A&M, and served as a first lieutenant and an infantry platoon leader in the 187th Infantry Division in Patton's Third Army. During the period of the Battle of the Bulge on the Western front, he was seriously wounded by a land mine, losing a leg and finding himself hospitalized for a year.

While a patient at the Bushnell General Hospital in Brigham City, Utah, one of his medical attendants was an attractive WAC surgical technician named Francille Lukens. A romance developed, and they were married in 1945, celebrating their fiftieth anniversary in 1995.

Sometime after Robert's 1949 graduation from law school, the father-son team joined with other partners in the establishment of the Midland Mortgage Company as half owners. Later, in 1963, when the other partners were contemplating expanding Midland into a multi-state operation, the Harrys, wishing to concentrate their entire activity in Oklahoma, sold their ownership stock and formed the Harry Mortgage Company. Later others in the family joined the company, which has remained until today a family-owned enterprise.

First to join was Robert's younger brother, Virgil M. Harry, Jr., who now serves as president of the company. Although more than four years younger, the junior Virgil has a background in many ways similar to Robert. Both served in World War II. Virgil came in near the end of the conflict, having enlisted to serve in the Army on his eighteenth birthday—the first day he was eligible.

Like his brother, Virgil also received a law degree, but after graduation chose a career in

❖

*Below: Bud and Robert Harry at the Harry Mortgage Company sign.*

*Bottom: Family members of Harry Mortgage Company at the sign in front of its new location are (from left to right) Steve Harry, Robert Harry, Bud Harry, Mark Harry, and Todd Harry.*

land development and construction, concentrating principally in building homes and apartment complexes. Later he joined his father and brother in starting Harry Mortgage Company. Robert's oldest son, Stephen, is now senior vice president of the company, while Mark is a vice president.

In his earlier years, Steve left college early to join the Oklahoma City Police Department. Later, while still serving with the department, he returned to college part-time and earned a Bachelor of Science Degree joining the company after graduation.

Steve's son, Todd, gives the Harry Mortgage Company its fourth generation. Todd is the systems administrator and is responsible for all software and hardware systems.

Robert's other son, Mark, oversees production and underwriting. Mark attended Oklahoma State University and received a degree in business administration.

Robert and Francille had three daughters all with Norwegian style names, influenced by their mother, who is of Norwegian origin. Kristen is a Ph.D., and a professor in psychology at Rose State College. Katrina, also a Ph.D., is a practicing psychologist. Their other daughter, Kimberly, along with her fifteen-month-old son, died from smoke inhalation in a tragic fire in 1988.

Virgil "Bud" Harry, Jr., has a son and daughter in the company. Virgil III is general counsel, while Sally Langer is vice president for accounting. Both graduating from the University of Oklahoma.

All three generations of the family have been active leaders in the Mortgage Bankers of America—the nation's principal trade association of the industry. Virgil, Sr. and Robert both served several years on its national board, and have certificates of commendation for their contributions to the industry. Steve is currently serving on the national board.

The family has also been active in the Christian churches (Disciples of Christ) in Oklahoma City. The older Virgil, during his lifetime, was an active leader in the Crown Heights Christian Church. Robert and Steve are active leaders in the Northwest Christian Church, both having served as board chairman, and Robert serving on the general board.

Despite the fact that the Harrys have resisted mergers or takeovers, the company has grown and prospered over the years. Harry Mortgage Company now has $200 million in outstanding loans, handled by 30 capable employees. It was a pioneer company in Oklahoma in introducing programs to save money for homebuyers. They are the first company in the state to introduce an interest-saving, biweekly home loan, providing substantial savings to the homeowner.

The company has also been a pioneer in offering a lease purchase bond program through which a family without resources for a down payment may purchase a home.

❖

*Top: Steve and Todd Harry check over records of a client.*

*Above: Mark (standing, left) and Steve Harry (standing, right) with Chairman Robert Harry.*

# EAGLE RIDGE INSTITUTE

Drive east on Northeast Sixty-third Street from Broadway Extension and, because of the wooded area to its front, you will probably not notice the handsome brick building behind the trees. Formerly the residence of the late oilman William T. Payne, it later became headquarters for his oil firm, Big Chief Drilling Company.

Within that building today, nestled in a forty-seven-acre tract, is the headquarters for Eagle Ridge Institute, known to many as ERI, an organization that may well be playing one of the most influential roles in Oklahoma County and beyond. ERI, a nonprofit social services agency dedicated to helping people and communities "soar," has grown from a single room in 1985 to a multi-center organization covering six counties, with more than one hundred highly skilled, dedicated professionals. ERI provides over a dozen programs and services, which impact more than one thousand individuals and families weekly.

John Mayfield, a divinity graduate, founded ERI in 1985. In 1989 Dr. Belinda Biscoe, a psychologist, and Carolyn Wakely, a licensed professional counselor, joined ERI as co-founders. The trio drafted ERI's mission to "promote healthy lifestyles for family preservation, youth development and community progress." Because Mayfield, Biscoe, and Wakely had observed substance abuse as the root of many youths' and families' problems, they integrated substance abuse education, prevention, and treatment as a major component in every ERI program.

Located at 601 Northeast Sixty-third Street, ERI's headquarters consist of the Area Prevention Resource Center, O'YES! youth development program, Oklahoma City Youth Council, FACES family strengthening program, and Therapeutic Foster Care program.

The Area Prevention Resource Center provides consultation and training to all ages,

helping them develop strategies to reduce substance abuse and other health threats.

O'YES! works toward delinquency prevention and gang intervention through case management to youth in the juvenile justice system.

The Oklahoma City Youth Council is self-governing with youth taking active roles in addressing challenges and developing leadership in the community.

The FACES family strengthening program serves middle school students and their families to reduce substance abuse and violence and increase the community's capacity to assist families.

Therapeutic Foster Care—which has sites in Oklahoma City, Wagoner, and McAlester—provides placement and therapeutic interventions to children who have been abused, neglected or have special needs.

Nearby, at 1401 Northeast Seventieth Street, is ERI's Adolescent Support Center, including a Parents as Partners in Education effort and an Eagle's Wings mentoring program. Parents as Partners in Education provide training to increase parents' knowledge and confidence in child-rearing activities and to enhance the developmental progress of children whose parents participate.

Eagle's Wings provides training and mentoring to youths who are at risk or involved in delinquency, substance abuse, or violence.

At 4420 North Lincoln, ERI provides outpatient substance abuse treatment for female welfare recipients and their families through the Bridge Builders program.

A Chance for Youth program provides after-school programs at Sooner Haven and Fred Factory Gardens apartments.

At ERI's Family Treatment Center in Guthrie, long-term residential treatment is provided for substance abusing women with their children, who receive therapeutic childcare. Clients also receive training in parenting and job skills.

ERI's board officers include Bruce Holmes, president; Bill Price, vice president; and Kelly Callahan, secretary/treasurer.

Believing in a continuum of care, ERI has many innovated programs and services to meet a variety of community needs. The agency is a proud contributor to the health and well being of Oklahomans.

✧
*Eagle Ridge Institute co-founders Belinda Biscoe, Ph.D., John Mayfield, and Carolyn Wakely.*

Variety Health Center, a nonprofit community-based health clinic serving the medical needs of low-income mothers and children in Oklahoma County, had its beginnings in the depths of the depression.

In 1932 the Oklahoma City Junior League established a health center in southeast Oklahoma City to provide low-cost medical services for pregnant women and their babies. Volunteer doctors, who were assisted by members of the Junior League, staffed the clinic.

In 1940 the Variety Club, a philanthropic organization of men in the entertainment field, dedicated to local and national healthcare needs, built a health center on South Hudson Street in Oklahoma City. They offered space to several healthcare agencies, one of which was the Junior League's maternal and child clinic. The new building was named the Variety Club Health Center, and the collection of agencies housed there was known as the Oklahoma County Health Association.

The center remained at this location until the late 1950s when the federal government announced that it had selected the clinic's site for the location of the new main post office. In 1961 a new Variety Health Center was built at Southwest Fourteenth Street and Walker, with an addition added in the early 1970s to meet the clinic's growing needs.

As healthcare costs rose in the 1980s, the need for Variety's services skyrocketed. More and more families found themselves without insurance, and turned to Variety for care. Still housed at the Fourteenth Street location, Variety's services by then included prenatal care, family planning, pregnancy testing, birthing classes, pediatric care, pediatric ophthalmology and dental clinics.

By the 1990s, it was clear that Variety's needs had outgrown its current space. More staff was involved in the day-to-day care of patients. More equipment and laboratory areas were needed. The building was no longer sufficient for the volume of patients Variety was seeing.

Variety soon embarked on a $1-million Capital Campaign for a new facility, which drew great support from the community. The Bank of Oklahoma generously donated a 13,500-square-foot building on Northwest Sixth Street for Variety's new home. Fundraising efforts provided for remodeling needs and the establishment of an endowment fund. Variety moved into its new facility in 1992.

Another successful Capital Campaign resulted in Variety's Mid-Del satellite clinic, which opened its doors in 1997 to better serve the healthcare needs of low-income mothers and children in the Midwest City/Del City area.

Today Variety Health Center provides prenatal care, family planning and pediatric care, including outreach and social services, to thousands each year. As always, Variety's fees are based on income. Nobody is denied care because of inability to pay.

Variety also provides nutritional services and food vouchers to pregnant and nursing women and their children through the WIC (Woman, Infants and Children) program. With several WIC sites in the Oklahoma City Metro Area, Variety is one of the largest WIC service providers in the State of Oklahoma.

Variety employs a largely full-time staff, including nurse practitioners and medical support personnel, and also enjoys a partnership with the OU MEDICAL CENTER, whose physicians and residents provide important services to the clinic.

Variety Health Center is committed to giving the best possible healthcare to those in need, and as Variety looks to the future, it anticipates more patients, more services, and more opportunities for growth as an organization helping people in our community who have few alternatives for affordable care.

✧

*Above: The Variety Health Center at 420 Northwest Sixth Street.*

*Below: Mothers and children, that's what Variety Health Center is all about.*

# ASSOCIATED COMMUNICATIONS AND RESEARCH SERVICES

Associated Communications and Research Services (ACRS) located at 817 Northeast Sixty-third Street was formed in 1987 to provide a comprehensive set of services to the independent telecommunication industry, creating a service center that combined several disciplines, in one firm, so that many services that require more than one consultant or vendor, can be accomplished by a single company. This was something unheard of in the independent telecommunications industry at the time.

Today, ACRS still provides a multitude of services to an extremely fast paced and ever-changing industry. ACRS' advantage is the ability to take an idea and carry it from concept to reality. Everything from engineering, construction and installation to financial analysis, regulatory reporting and asset valuation are offered by a staff of 50 seasoned professionals. ACRS is currently offering services to over 30 telecommunications companies throughout the United States, from the more traditional land line companies to more specialized optical high speed data networks supplying competitive voice, data, and video services.

Clay Curtis, whose background consists of over twenty years of telecommunications experience with Southwestern Bell and Bellcore, established ACRS. Curtis is a native of Oklahoma who received a Bachelor of Science from Central State University and a Masters of Business Administration from Oklahoma City University and is a registered professional engineer in 7 states with reciprocity in the other 41 contiguous states. Curtis had worked with the independent telecommunication industry, at Southwestern Bell, as the Toll Pool administrator from 1985 to 1987. In this capacity, Curtis was responsible for the administration of a $230-million pool that provided higher cost, rural telephone companies the ability to offer comparable services as that offered in larger cities, and at comparable costs.

After starting ACRS, they were afforded the opportunity to design the first light wave digital interactive educational system in the United States. The result was a fiber network connecting rural schools and one university into a single interactive network that allowed many of the smaller schools to offer classes that couldn't be offered before but were required by North Central Accreditation. Also, in 1996, ACRS designed and constructed a 65-mile educational network in southeastern Oklahoma connecting rural schools to a local college.

In 1989 ACRS assisted the Gila River Indian Community, south of Phoenix, Arizona, in procuring their own certification to offer telecommunication services within the Reservation boundaries. The community was formerly served by U.S. West, and the cost of providing service to many of the members of the community was cost prohibitive, which was also antiquated and of poor quality. The first subscribers were provided service in the summer of 1989, and by 1995; the entire reservation was served with state-of-the-art telecommunications services. ACRS assisted in not only the consultation services for the procurement of existing facilities but also engineered the network and provided the financial services and regulatory functions to get the new company off to a promising start. In addition to the Gila River Indian Community, ACRS assisted the Fort Mojave Indian Reservation in a similar venture and by 1992; this system was serving its first subscribers.

Since the early 1990s, ACRS has expanded its offering to include wireless network design, installation of lightwave and frame relay electronics as well as telecommunications and pipeline construction. Since 1997, ACRS is providing site acquisition services for wireless service providers, in addition to maintaining its existing service platform. ACRS continues to expand with a second generation of ACRS professionals, including Clay's Sons Sam and Charles Curtis, and Lila Crossfield his only daughter, to bring the highest quality services to the telecommunications industry in assisting its clientele in meeting the challenges of the future.

❖

*Clay Curtis, founder and president of Associated Communications and Research Services.*

# CATTLEMEN'S STEAKHOUSE

"Oklahoma City: Where Beef Reigns Supreme" was the title of a feature story in *Gourmet Magazine*, a leading national publication in the field of food service.

The story tells of several outstanding restaurants in Oklahoma City, which give the city a national reputation for fine beef dinners.

It is not at all surprising that the first mentioned and the most generously praised, was Cattlemen's Steakhouse, adjacent to the Oklahoma City stockyards. This is because Cattlemen's has a reputation, which has attracted presidents and governors, motion picture and television celebrities, as well as top business leaders of the nation. Cattlemen's is also the most continuously operated restaurant in Oklahoma County.

The restaurant opened with the coming of the city's first national industry, the Morris Packing Company, which later became Armour and Company. This 1910 arrival began Oklahoma's reputation as a major center in the livestock industry and the beginning of Stockyards City.

Set apart from downtown in a period before mass ownership of automobiles, the area east of the stockyards was filled with restaurants and small hotels. The most popular and the only remaining of those restaurants is Cattlemen's on Agnew, just north of Southwest Fifteenth Street. Today, lacking less than a single decade of being a century old, Cattlemen's is even more popular than it was in the heyday of the stockyards era.

It was Cattlemen's restaurant where President George H. W. Bush, then running for reelection, was taken on his visit to Oklahoma City. Frequent visitors among celebrities, when they come to Oklahoma City, are Reba McIntyre, Garth Brooks, and Michael Martin Murphy, to name just a few. It is believed that every governor of Oklahoma has dined at Cattlemen's at least once, and some many times.

Although the restaurant has changed hands a few times during its ninety-plus years, its specialties and its reputation have had few changes. Today it is best known, both locally and nationally, for beef, lamb fries, and its unique salad dressing.

Dick Stubbs took over the restaurant on a lease-purchase arrangement in 1989, completing the purchase in the early 1990s.

Stubbs has been a leader, both in Oklahoma and nationally, in restaurant associations. His service spans many years on the board of directors of the Oklahoma Restaurant Association as well as the national association, and he remains an honorary member of the national board. He spent twelve years on the Oklahoma City Convention and Visitors Bureau. He has been a board member and is past president of the Stockyards City Main Street Program. He is on the advisory board to the college of Human Environmental Sciences of Oklahoma State University.

Stubbs is particularly proud of the work of the Stockyards Main Street Program, which was the first urban Main Street Program area west of the Mississippi River. When the program was started, the Stockyards area had many boarded up commercial buildings, resulting, in part, from a shift farther south of shopping areas. Consumer trade was down, including that of the Cattlemen's Restaurant. Today, largely through the Main Street Program effort, in which Stubbs played a major role, new businesses have sprung up in the stockyards area. As for Cattlemen's, its business is the highest in its history.

✧

*An early picture of Cattlemen's Steakhouse, which remains in its original location in south Oklahoma City.*

# BEAM'S INDUSTRIES, INC.

Ada Foree Beam remembers the hard work and undaunting perseverance her husband had as he dreamed of starting his own business in Oklahoma City. An east Texas boy with a keen business mind, Orville Thomas Beam, known by friends and family as Tom, had worked his way through the Depression era as a clerk in the Civil Conservation Corp. of the 1930s and had recently been transferred to Oklahoma City by the National Park Service. A job at the Goodyear Tire Company piqued his interest, and Tom and Ada were ready to settle down. The innovative "Help Yourself" service stations were quickly becoming popular around the country, and Tom joined a partner in opening a station at the corner of Thirteenth and Robinson.

Automobile accessories such as seat covers and seat belts were a novelty at the time, and Tom decided to buy a few patents and add a seat covering business to the station. Tom and Ada loved the work and decided to buy out their partner, took out the gas pumps, and opened Beam's Seat Cover Center in the early 1950s. With little competition and a love for cars, the Beams' would put seat covers in nearly every car on the streets of Oklahoma City in the 1940s, '50s, and '60s.

As his business grew and prospered, Tom became interested in an accessory making its way into automobiles across the country—the seat belt. Intrigued with the idea, Tom began manufacturing and selling seat belts in the 1960s. Advertisements for the accessories included "A Beam's belt, the safest thing around

you" and "You can't buy better protection...To save your life! A Beam's premium Auto Safety Belt." Seat belts would soon become the focus of Beam's Industries, Inc., and the Beams had found their most successful enterprise just beginning.

The success of the business enabled the company to grow as well as allow the Beam's to make contributions to their church, the Church of Christ. Tom and Ada have been strong supporters of Oklahoma Christian University throughout the years, and the OC Library was named after them in honor of their support. As Tom once mentioned to one of his attorneys, "I live to give."

Tom and Ada's commitment to the Church of Christ brought them in touch with a missionary to Germany who asked them to consider adopting three children in the area. Gerd Fecht, Dieter, and Edgar joined the Beam family and made their way to America and a new home in Oklahoma City in 1955. Over the years the children were involved both at the Seat Cover Center as well as at the seatbelt manufacturing company. Presently Gerd Fecht, along with his son-in-law Frank Smith, and Ted Merritt, directs the manufacturing, distribution, and sales of seatbelts for a variety of applications worldwide. Two decades after the company moved its headquarters from the location at Thirteenth and Robinson to I-40 and Villa, Beam's Industries is now located on South Sunnylane in Oklahoma City.

Through the years, Tom and Ada were also involved in real estate development, including the Bavarian Forest, Dutch Forest, and Lake Highlands developments in the Edmond area. Ada still resides in this area.

*Above: Ada and Tom Beam in 1957.*

*Below: The original "Beams" in 1955 at North Thirteenth and Robinson.*

Ten years ago, John M. Howard retired for the second time. His first retirement was from the United States Air Force, where he had served with distinction for twenty-one years and had attained the rank of major. His second retirement was from the Federal Aviation Administration, where he had spent more than twenty years, climaxing as director for Aviation Standards at the Mike Monroney Aeronautical Center.

It didn't take him long walking the malls and enjoying a leisurely life to decide retirement wasn't for him, and at age sixty-one he began his third career as an entrepreneur in the aviation industry with Aero Tech Services Associates.

Today he is president of Aero Tech Service Associates New Aero Tech Inc., providing technical services to governmental and private segments of the aviation industry throughout the country.

The story of John Howard is one of industry and determination to perform well and to succeed. He spent his first thirteen years in a coalmining village in the hills of West Virginia before moving with his parents to a farm in Southeastern Ohio.

Abandoning farming upon graduation from high school, Howard joined the U.S. Air Force, with hopes of becoming a pilot. However, he was rejected for pilot school because of his age and lack of sufficient education. After a brief tour in Alaska, he continued in his effort to obtain pilot training. Eventually he was accepted for the Aviation Cadet program, and in August 1954, he was commissioned a Second Lieutenant and received his pilot wings.

His career continued with duties as communications and electronics officer and multi-engine jet pilot. He retired after twenty-one years service with the rank of major. Within a week after retirement Howard was back on duty again, this time as a civil servant with the Federal Aviation Administration (FAA) assigned to Japan with the Tokyo Flight Inspection Group, serving countries in the Pacific and Far East.

Howard was later transferred to the FAA Washington headquarters as chief of the Washington Aircraft Management Branch.

Among other things, this provided him the opportunity to pursue, on his own time, a college degree. Enrolling at American University, he pursued and eventually obtained a master's degree without benefit of a bachelor degree.

Howard was subsequently transferred to the Mike Monroney Aeronautical Center in Oklahoma City, where be became deputy director and later director of the Aviation Standards National Field Office. He retired with twenty-and-a-half years FAA service in December 1990.

Aero Tech Service Associates (ATSA), Inc. began in 1992 as a one-man operation in his own home. The company provides aviation related services, including technical training, systems and information technology, aircraft and program management services, system engineering services, telecommunications service, aircraft maintenance base operations support, and other aviation related services.

ATSA's corporate headquarters is located south of the I-40 and Meridian intersection. The aviation industry, both governmental and in the private sector, are fortunate that John Howard chose not to stop after his second retirement.

✧

*John M. Howard, founder and president of Aero Tech Service Associates.*

# HERITAGE LAW CENTER

Drive along the south end of Heritage Hills and you may be impressed by a two-story Victorian style home at 515 Northwest 13th Street, just west of Walker. The house has historical significance. It was built in 1911 and first occupied by Moses and Minnie Herskowitz, who founded and operated the Aurora Bargain Store, selling clothing and located on the corner of Grand and Broadway.

Today it is occupied by the Heritage Law Center, the offices of E. Elaine Schuster, who has retained the historical appearance of the building, both exterior and interior, and her office is the former dining room. Sealed into lavatory fixtures are historical artifacts of a bygone period, found by Elaine when she purchased the home. Included is a 1920 Oklahoma Income Tax receipt, showing a total tax of $3.20, paid by John Rinehart.

Elaine Schuster brings into her practice a wide range of legal experience. Armed with her law degree, she practiced with Whitten & Whitten. Then she joined the staff of the district attorney, working with Curtis Harris and Andy Coats. For three years she was head of the civil division. Her experience has also included work with another private firm before forming her own professional corporation and Heritage Law Center.

Elaine is a third generation American. Her grandfather came to the United States from Bavaria, Germany, just prior to the Civil War. Her grandmother came from England. Elaine's father, John O. Schuster, completed his fifth-grade education in East Texas before being apprenticed at a machine shop until he was seventeen. After working in Virginia and Colorado, he and his wife, Eula, returned to Oklahoma City in 1931, and established General Machine Works, an oil field machine shop on Southeast Twenty-ninth Street, and A&A Tool & Supply, a used equipment sales company. It was in Oklahoma City that Elaine was born and reared. Her brother, Campbell, operated General Machine Works after her father's retirement. Both Campbell and John, Elaine's brothers, are deceased.

Elaine was graduated from Classen High School before attending and graduating from Sweet Briar College in Virginia. She earned a master's degree at the University of Oklahoma, taught economics at Southeastern State University in Durant before entering the University of Oklahoma College of Law.

Schuster has served her community in many ways. She was one of the founding members of the National Kidney Foundation of Oklahoma in 1969 and she has been a member of the Metro Tech Career-Technical School District Board of Education since 1982, first appointed by Governor George Nigh. She also does committee work with the Oklahoma City Community Foundation.

She was elected the first woman elder of University Place Christian Church, and is now a deacon at Crown Heights Christian Church. In these and other ways she has followed her family tradition of always being willing to give back to the community.

*Above: E. Elaine Schuster.*

*Below: This turn of the century style home is headquarters to the Heritage Law Center and attorney E. Elaine Schuster.*

In 1900 a few dedicated Free Methodist women evangelists responded with Christian concern to the plight of unwed pregnant girls. These ladies garnered the support of leading Oklahomans, including the Territorial Governor William M. Jenkins, and his wife, to form the first organization in the Territory established to minister to these women and their babies.

The Oklahoma Rescue Home, (later Holmes Home of Redeeming Love, Home of Redeeming Love and Deaconess Home), broadened its vision by moving from Guthrie to Oklahoma City in 1910. The ladies and staff sacrificed, often without pay, and solicited gifts to sustain their work.

They farmed their forty acres and lived off the farm products. The ministry expanded to include a Deaconess training program, nurses training and a residence for needy women. But the focus of their love remained the unwed mothers.

A natural outgrowth of the Home's mission was a freestanding facility to provide pregnancy care. In 1931 the first medical facility of 22 beds was constructed, later expanding to 45 beds. It became a general hospital named Deaconess in 1944. Pioneering the latest medical innovations, it was the first Oklahoma hospital specifically dedicated to family practice medicine. Deaconess had several other firsts in Oklahoma such as the first intensive care unit, outpatient surgery center, remote monitoring of EKGs, senior diagnostic psychiatric facility, and the only lithotripsy facility in western Oklahoma. Deaconess was also the first Oklahoma City hospital to open a single birthing room unit.

The history of the first century of Deaconess is interwoven with the family of Anna L. Witteman, the superintendent of the Home, and later the first administrator of Deaconess Hospital, from 1901 to 1951. Her nephew, Ralph E. Butterfield served as Home superintendent along with his wife, Gladys, until their retirement in 1975. Under his leadership, a critical care unit, a new Home facility, outpatient surgery facility, and two hospital additions were completed, increasing capacity from 45 to 177 inpatient beds.

His son-in-law, Melvin J. Spencer, who served as administrator until January 1992, succeeded Butterfield. During his tenure, major progress included the lithotripsy facility, radiation oncology, the senior diagnostic center, Copper Lake retirement facility, two physician's office buildings, and an increase in capacity to 250 beds.

The leadership and vision of the board of directors and chief executive officers, John Ellis (1992-1996) and Paul Dougherty (1996 to present) are responsible for the major recent advancements at Deaconess Hospital, which remains the only healthcare facility in greater Oklahoma City not affiliated with another healthcare entity.

Today Deaconess treats patients from throughout Oklahoma and beyond in inpatient, outpatient and emergency settings. New programs and services joining Deaconess Pregnancy and Adoption Services (formerly Deaconess Home) have been added, such as the Wound Care Center, Healthy Heart Center, and outreach laboratory and radiology services. The twenty-first century sees Deaconess prepared for the future with a convenient medical mall with services patients need most located within close proximity. Major hospital remodeling and the new Deaconess at Bethany facility that includes mental health services have increased the licensed bed size to 313.

Deaconess Hospital is firmly committed to its unchanging mission of providing physical, mental and spiritual needs to patients who seek healing from its excellent nursing care and high-tech facilities, and, above all, genuine Christian compassion and love.

❖

*Above: Deaconess has grown from humble origins, evolving into a major healthcare provider.*

*Below: A few of the thousands of precious lives rescued by the Deaconess ladies.*

# MALCOLM HALL PROPERTIES

❖

*Malcolm Hall in front of his newest development.*

Meet Malcolm Hall, and not long into your visit you will realize he is an unusual and interesting individual.

Most likely you will find him in blue jeans and work shirt at a construction job site, planning, consulting or helping out in the building, enlarging or remodeling of a commercial or industrial structure.

You will not realize immediately that he is a man with two degrees in economics, and an attorney, and is licensed by the state as a mechanical contractor, a heating and air conditioning contractor and pipe fitter.

But these are only a few of his activities. Aside from building and limited legal work, he is a Scoutmaster, a church leader, a Sunday School teacher, and, for thirteen years, was a children's baseball coach.

Malcolm is a native of Ballinger, Texas. He attended Texas A&M University, where he was president of the student body, then as a Hagan Fellow, followed by the University of Kentucky, where he earned additional degrees in economics. He was soon caught up in the Vietnam War, assigned to counter-intelligence.

Following the war, he attended the University of Oklahoma Law School and served on the Oklahoma Law Review, made up of the top six students in the class. Following graduation, he opened his own law office and married the former Judy Colclaser of Oklahoma City.

His interest in building physical things never changed, despite the years of studying economics and law. His new career as a builder began when he purchased repossessed warehouses from Southwestern Bank, and began renovation.

Next came apartment building, leading to the construction of twenty-eight hundred apartments. Hall then began building warehouses and distribution centers.

Hall caters his efforts to the entrepreneurial pioneer spirit, which he believes is the key to the American economic system. He reasons that a large segment of the population has the dream of owning and operating a business. Those who pursue the dream desire office space, often with storefront, and it is to help the entrepreneur seek that dream that Hall's construction efforts are directed.

Does he still practice law? Well, sort of. The word "attorney" remains after his name in the telephone directory, and he admits being in court a few times each year. However, his legal interest is usually confined to helping people.

A strong believer in the "right to life," Hall has provided the legal work for persons desiring adoptions free of charge ever since he opened his law office in 1968.

Malcolm and Judy have five children, ranging from 13 to 31 years of age. The youngest, Houston, is a member of Boy Scout Troop 555 at Heritage Hall School, where Malcolm serves as its Scoutmaster. Malcolm and Houston have been inducted into the Order of the Arrow, a Scouting honor society.

Hall is a board member and chairman of the worship music committee of Westminster Presbyterian Church, a Sunday School teacher for thirty years, a board member of the Texas Presbyterian Foundation and is chairman of the board of Mo-Ranch, the largest church camp and conference center in North America.

He and his company have received the annual Partnership Award of Goodwill Industries for their service in helping in the recovery of the handicapped.

Lawyer...builder...developer...youth leader...coach...church leader...civic leader? Take your choice. That's Malcolm Hall.

"Find a need and fill it" describes the key to success in this business. This is the basis of the success of Joe Vanlandingham, and of the company he founded and leads, Presort First Class.

A visit to his plant at 2832 Southeast Ninth Street, and watching machines read addresses and sort letters at the rate of thirty-six thousand each hour, would almost blow the mind of even the most sophisticated technologist. But what is even more amazing is that one man in his own backyard garage started it all.

Vanlandingham went to work as a letter carrier for the Postal Service in 1966. While working for the Post Office, he graduated from the University of Central Oklahoma in 1969. At that time he had no idea where his postal experience might lead him.

In his position as customer service representative, he was given the assignment of promoting among business customers the presorting of mail by zip code. This enabled lowering the postal delivery cost to the customer, and at the same time saving the postal system the cost of sorting the heavy volume of mail that passes through each day.

Business executives often pointed out to him that the additional sorting cost to the company exceeded the postal savings and that there was a need for an organization specializing in sorting.

Vanlandingham decided he would attempt to fill that need himself. He formed his own company, using his garage for headquarters, and with no employees. Initially, he had a single customer—Liberty National Bank. Others soon followed, and employees were hired. Five years and two locations later, he purchased his present headquarters building at 2832 Southeast Ninth Street and currently employs 82 people, serving 210 customers.

As the company grew, so did the expanding ZIP Marking by the Post Office and the technology of the industry. Today an eleven-digit bar code matches each letter to a specific letter carrier. The letter sorting machines print the bar code and drop the letter into a tray assigned to that bar code. The company leases a nationwide database of addresses from the Post Office.

Mailing letters through Presort First Class can save money, even for companies that have their own equipment for sorting. This is because the postal rate becomes lower as the number of letters in a single zip code tray increases. Also in first class mail, it is not necessary that all letters in presorted bundles come from the same organization. Thus, each barcoded bundle may contain letters from many companies mixed together and mailed at the rate offered for the number of letters in the bundle. Presort First Class comingles the mail of all customers, maximizing the finest sortation while allowing customers the lowest discount and best service on their mail.

The reduced postal rate does not even require that letters be in the same size envelopes, and the sorting machines at Presort First Class can easily sort mixed-sized envelopes. For these reasons, both large and smaller companies can save money through the mass presort procedure.

Joe Vanlandingham is recognized nationally in the industry and is serving his second term as secretary of the National Association of Presort Mailers.

✧

*This assembly line style machine at Presort First Class reads addresses and sorts letters at the rate of thirty-six thousand each hour.*

# LEE WAY MOTOR FREIGHT

One of the most prominent and recognized trucking companies from the late 1930s through 1976 was Lee Way Motor Freight. Founded by R. W. "Whitt" Lee, it began in 1934 as an expansion of Lee's taxi and bus service.

A homesteader of Custer County in 1901, Young Whitt Lee left school as a teenager to move to Clinton to work in the used car business. He soon began his entrepreneurial path by operating his own one-man taxi service. This he expanded into a bus line serving small towns in western Oklahoma. He moved to Oklahoma City and began his trucking career by purchasing two trucks for hauling between Oklahoma City and Amarillo.

His bus line flourished, but Lee found trucking more to his liking. So he sold the bus business to Greyhound in the early 1940s and thereafter concentrated on the trucking firm. In spite of the Depression, the company expanded. It continued to grow through the wartime period, providing long haul service for general commodities. During the same period Lee developed a subsidiary company for short hauls, serving every part of Oklahoma.

Oklahoma City Chamber of Commerce and was a national board member of the American Trucking Association. He was president of the Associated Motor Carriers of Oklahoma and was instrumental in the formation of Transport Insurance Company, headquartered in Dallas. Thirty years after his death in 1970, the Oklahoma City/County Historical Society posthumously recognized him as a "Pathmaker" of Oklahoma County.

Lee's sons and daughter have also been active in Oklahoma City community affairs, particularly in the cultural area.

Bob Lee served as president of the Oklahoma City Chamber of Commerce, vice president of the Jaycees and was on the boards of the Oklahoma City Art Center and the Allied Arts Foundation. He died in 1989.

Stanley Lee served as president of the Science and Arts and Allied Arts Foundations, and was a leader in the Chamber of Commerce, Omniplex Science Museum and the Oklahoma City Art Center. He was president of the Oklahoma City YMCA for five years.

Betty Lou Lee Upsher has served on the boards of the Oklahoma City Art Center, Oklahoma City Zoo, and the Junior League of Oklahoma City.

There are now ten third generation members of the family, all of who are in some way active in their communities. No doubt the fourth and fifth generations will continue in the spirit of the Lee Way.

❖
*Above: R. W. "Whitt" Lee.*

*Below: An early Lee Way Motor Freight delivery truck.*

Lee retired in the mid-1960s. His sons, Robert E. Lee and M. Stanley Lee, both of whom had been with the company since the close of World War II, took over management and continued to expand the company. When Lee Way was sold to Pepsi-Cola in 1976, it employed 3,595 people, had revenues of $115 million and covered some 25,000 miles.

Lee was an active community leader. He served on the board of directors of the

Perhaps no facility brought Oklahoma City more into the national limelight than the almost-forgotten Delmar Garden—a 140-acre amusement park, established in the city when only 13 years old.

Those who brought it about were brothers John and Peter Sinopoulo, who emigrated from Sparta, Greece. They chose this pioneer community to build a fantastic park extending south and west from Western. The park, which they named Delmar Garden, opened in 1902.

The park featured a multi-story restaurant and beer garden, a hotel, and the most sophisticated thrill rides of the turn of the century. There were racing tracks for horses and automobiles. John L. Sullivan, the world's most famous bare knuckle fighter of all time, fought in the boxing ring. The Apache Indian Warrior often paroled from imprisonment at Fort Sill, signed autographs at Delmar for ten cents each.

The National Editorial Convention and an attempted statehood convention were held at Delmar Garden in 1905. In the 1909 season, Delmar closed but the Sinopoulo brothers were not through with amusement business.

In 1910 they purchased the Overholser Opera House on West Grand, which they converted into the Orpheum Theater. Nationwide entertainment was brought to the city through the Orpheum circuit. Later they built an outdoor motion picture theater, called the Airdrome.

Other theaters they acquired or built included the Dreamland on Main Street; the Empress on West Grand; the Folly, also on Grand; and the Lyric on Robinson Street where the First National Center would later be built.

In the early 1920s, the theaters of the city banded together to form the Midwest Enterprise Company, with John Sinopoulo as chairman and Peter as president.

In 1928 the Sinopoulos sold their theater business to Warner Brothers, but retained the real estate and moved into the oil and real estate business, once owning 170 pieces of property in Oklahoma City. They built the St. George Greek Orthodox Church and were major investors in the Biltmore Hotel and the Midwest Building.

As World War II approached, the brothers joined the war effort, devoting time and resources to Savings Bond campaigns and war relief.

After the war they wanted to give back to the country that had nurtured their earliest days. Thus, they formed a charitable foundation in Athens, Greece. The Foundation has developed a church, two schools, a cemetery, a 5,000-seat amphitheater, a park, a library for study of art and drama, and other facilities, principally in or near their childhood community of Sparta.

Peter Sinopoulo died in 1955, but John lived to the age of 101. One of John's last public events took place when he attended the dedication of the Bicentennial Plaza in Oklahoma City's Civic Center, where one of the historic markers featured the history of entertainment in Oklahoma City. At the top of the granite monument is an engraved drawing of Delmar Garden—the most famous entertainment complex in Oklahoma City's history.

✧

*Left: John Sinopoulo.*

*Right: Peter Sinopoulo.*

# DATA MONITOR SYSTEMS

It has often been said that failure can sometimes lead to success.

Perhaps an unexpected and unplanned example of this is a failure, which indirectly led to the founding and success of Data Monitor Systems at 1120 South Douglas Boulevard in Midwest City.

William L. "Bill" Harper, who founded the company, was a career non-commissioned officer in the United States Air Force from 1949 until 1969. Late in his career he was trained by the military in computer technology when he flunked the portion of his course, which dealt with documentation and flow-charting.

Instead of giving up the course, he found himself digging into the subject, perhaps deeper than anyone who had attended the course. In 1979 he wrote a paper on the subject of computer programming documentation, and sent it to a national trade journal for publishing consideration. Upon examining the article, the editor of the journal insisted that Harper enlarge on the subject to prepare a book on documentation. Unknown as an author, he resisted this challenge. However, the editor insisted. Finally, he took it on, and spent nearly two years in study, research and writing the text.

The text was eventually sent to the Prentice Hall Company, one of the top publishers in the nation, and to Harper's surprise, it was accepted. His book, *Documentation: Standards and Procedures*, soon became the standard text in its field, and later moved into a second edition. Harper quickly became recognized as a national authority on documentation.

Upon his retirement from the Air Force as a master sergeant, he joined Futuronics Corporation, a New York firm and government service contractor, with an office in Oklahoma, providing communications equipment to the government and the private sector. While employed with the New York firm he obtained local contracts with the Postal Services Technical Training Center in Norman. He later realized that his New York employer was facing almost immediate bankruptcy. When Harper learned that the company was not prepared to financially handle the contract, he was given permission to proceed on his own. Thus, his company, Data Monitor Systems, was formed, providing classroom instructions in electronics for the Postal employees.

Because the company initially was small and slow in growth, Harper later disassociated from his active leadership and joined the Civil Service staff at Tinker Air Force Base. There he was involved with computer communications until retiring in 1984.

It was that year that Harper rejoined Data Monitor Systems, which then had only three employees. The company has since grown to 240 employees in 13 states, extending east and west from Pennsylvania to Colorado and north and south from Wisconsin to Florida.

However, growth was not automatic. It was only after two years following Harper's rejoining the company that he personally drew a salary from his own firm. Today the firm produces revenues of more than eight million dollars annually. The company deals entirely in government contracts, and currently has contracts exceeding $25 million.

Data Monitor Systems, which started in Norman in 1975, moved to the Atkinson Plaza in the former Midwest City First National Bank Building in 1986, and to its present location in Midwest City's Regional Square at 1120 South Douglas Boulevard in 1995.

When we visit the remodeled Civic Center Music Hall, watch the Redhawks at the Bricktown Ball Park, or attend a function at the Waterford Hotel, we are well aware of the attractiveness of the facilities. However, we seldom give a thought to the underlying structural systems of these buildings.

Without carefully engineered structures, beautiful facades and comfortable interiors cannot exist. The detailed planning that holds a building together is the responsibility of structural engineers. In the case of all of the above-mentioned facilities, the structural plans were developed by Zahl-Ford, Inc., of Oklahoma City, one of the leading structural engineering companies of the Southwest.

Zahl-Ford, Inc., located at 8411 South Walker, also provided the stuctural engineering design for the Omnidome at the Kirkpatrick Center, Epworth Villa retirement home, St. Elijah Eastern Orthodox and St. George Greek Orthodox churches, along with the remodeling and enlargement of First United Methodist Church. Zahl-Ford also designed the building structure for the Donald W. Reynolds Visual Arts Center in downtown Oklahoma City. In 1983, Leadership Square was designed as a joint venture project between Zahl-Ford and another local firm.

The company has designed buildings ranging geographically from Florida to Hawaii, and its principals have engineering registration in numerous states. The founding principals in the corporation are Robert C. Zahl, president, and J. Stephen Ford, executive vice president. The company is made up of 14 people, 9 of whom are graduate engineers. Current ownership includes several of these employees.

Although the company may be best known for the buildings they designed or remodeled, nearly half of their projects deal with the inspection of damaged or deteriorating structures. Among them has been the evaluation of more than 400 buildings, damaged either in the April 19, 1995 federal building bombing, or from the May 3, 1999 tornado.

What is the most challenging project the company has ever faced? Both Zahl and Ford agree that it was the Oklahoma City's Civic Center Music Hall renovation. This project was literally the construction of a building within a building. Most of the floors, including the stage, were removed from the mid-1930s structure, leaving little more than the outer walls and roof. The biggest challenge came in providing temporary stability to the remaining portions of the building during the reconstruction.

Zahl-Ford has received a number of honors, both state and national, and its principals have been leaders in several technical and business associations. Ford has authored numerous articles on reinforced concrete columns, frame analysis and construction inspection, and has received the American Concrete Institute Wason Medal for the Most Meritorious Paper.

Zahl is currently serving a six-year appointment on the Oklahoma State Board of Registration for Professional Engineers and Land Surveyors, and on NCEES, the organization that produces the licensing examinations for the engineering profession.

# ZAHL-FORD, INC.

❖

*Above: Civic Center Music Hall.*

*Below: Bricktown Ballpark.*

# DeLong Mailing Service

Carden James "Cookie" DeLong literally started a career as a young boy in Reading, Pennsylvania, which eventually led to one of the country's leading mailing companies. As a youth he delivered newspapers in his hometown at a time when one carrier would deliver all papers serving the area, sometimes even 'throwing' papers from the moving trolley or train. Some of his customers were Milton Hershey, William Wrigley, and the Luden and Smith Brothers (cough drop fame). While waiting for his papers, DeLong often helped the mailers prepare and address the papers to be mailed.

Although underage for military service in World War I, DeLong fooled the induction officers and soon was overseas. While in France he made friends with three men from Oklahoma City and decided to visit them after the war. He never returned home, finding employment with his friends in the print industry in Oklahoma City.

They often worked five or six shifts per week, doing four or five shifts on Friday and Saturday, allowing time for contracting their own jobs during the week. While working for the *Daily Oklahoman*, DeLong met Gertrude Brown, one of the "cookies" walking by at lunch, and whom he later married. He earned his nickname by calling the girls 'cookies'—a term he picked up in France.

DeLong contracted for and mailed many papers over the years, traveling to whichever print shop earned the bid. The Rural Electric Cooperative is still a customer of the company. Others include Farm Bureau, Farmers Union, American Legion, Veterans of Foreign Wars and many more.

As times changed so did the mailing process, from lists printed on galleys, cut, pasted together, and applied by hand-held machine, to e-mail lists and ink jet machines, addressing thousands per hour.

While most of the company's clients are in central Oklahoma, a few are foreign and national. They come from New York, Florida, Nebraska and Colorado, to name a few. Frank Maschino, Delong's son-in-law, joined the company in 1963, and was one of five full-time employees. By 1989, when Maschino purchased the company, the firm had grown to nearly fifty full-time employees.

In April 2001 Frank Maschino sold DeLong Mailing Service to The Oklahoma Publishing Company. The new company, Oklahoma Direct, has added strategic marketing services to the mail-processing business. These services provide an analytical tool to help advertisers realize a greater return on their investment.

The Oklahoma City/County Historical Society, publisher of *Historic Oklahoma County*, was organized twenty years ago to preserve and spotlight the history of this central Oklahoma area. During its existence the society completed a study of historical structures of the county, published three books, and organized and developed two museums. The Oklahoma City/County Historical Society raised more money than any other organization toward placing of names of Oklahoma war deceased on the war memorial monument in the State Capitol Complex.

An early project of the Oklahoma City/County Historical Society was making a detailed survey of historical structures in Oklahoma County. This resulted in the first book to be published by the Society, *The Physical Legacy of Oklahoma County*.

Two other books have been published by the Society. They are *Heart of the Promised Land: A History of Oklahoma County*, issued eighteen years ago, and *The Central Theme*, a history of Oklahoma High School, which became Central High School in Oklahoma City. *Historic Oklahoma County* makes the Society's fourth book.

In 1985 the Society developed an Oklahoma County Museum, named the Museum of the Unassigned Lands, and operated it for ten years before the company, which had furnished the museum space, had to retrench its operation, and the space was no longer available. However, the museum exhibits are in storage and will be seen again in 2004 in the new Oklahoma History Center in the State Capitol Complex, where the Society will have office and exhibit space.

The Society recently obtained projection equipment, and will be preparing a video program on Oklahoma County history to be shown to organizations, including school groups, who will be visiting the new center.

The Central High School Museum is, located in the Southwestern Bell state headquarters building—once Oklahoma City's Central High School. Originally called Oklahoma High School, this was the first high school in Oklahoma County. As the city grew and new high schools opened, its name was changed to Central High School. This museum interprets the history of the county's first high school, and displays many artifacts from the past.

The Society produces two quarterly publications. One is a news publication for its membership. The other, known as *The War Chief*, is an eight-page publication of

historical features by members of the Indian Territory Posse of Oklahoma Westerners—a Western history organization which will share offices with the Society in the new history center. This publication also goes to libraries and colleges throughout the state.

A major annual event of the Society is its annual Pathmaker luncheon, in which four living and four deceased residents or natives of Oklahoma County are honored for lasting contributions to the county, city, and state. They will be recognized with plaques and files in the new Oklahoma History Center, now under construction in the State Capitol Complex.

# OKLAHOMA CITY/COUNTY HISTORICAL SOCIETY

❖

*The officers of the Oklahoma City/County Historical Society (from left to right): Paul Matthews, president; Carolyn Hubbard, first vice president; Kerry Kratchmer, second vice president; and William D. Welge, treasurer. Not pictured is Mary Jeanne Hansen, secretary.*

# ACP
## SHEET METAL
## COMPANY

❖

*Harold Dills, president of ACP.*

When we walk into a cooled building in the summertime, or a heated building during winter, we seldom perceive the air conditioning and heating system beyond the opening in the wall. But there is much more than that. Each duct is carefully engineered and tailor-made for the building it serves. This is the challenge which ACP Sheet Metal Company faces every day.

ACP builds ventilation systems for many major organizations, including hospitals, schools and theatres.

Its founder and president is Harold Dills, a North Carolina native assigned by the military to Tinker Air Force Base, where he met and married Claudette Patten. His father-in-law introduced him to the sheet metal industry in 1960, and he established his own company in 1977.

ACP began as a one-man operation and now covers twenty-one thousand square feet. It prides itself on state-of-the-art technology.

ACP has completed a wide range of projects in four states, including the duct system for the Museum of Natural History at the University of Oklahoma.

Dills served four years on the national board of directors for the Sheet Metal Air Conditioning National Association, and has been president of the National Environmental Balancing Bureau. He is an elder at the Edmond Church of Christ.

Entering business in recent years is his daughter, Patrice Dills Douglas, who serves as vice president of ACP. She is a graduate of Oklahoma Christian University and the University of Oklahoma College of Law. She served ten years as attorney for the Oklahoma Supreme Court. She is a graduate of Leadership Oklahoma City.

---

## SLEEPY
## HOLLOW

❖

*Sleepy Hollow Restaurant is nestled in the woods on Northeast Fiftieth Street.*

Remember the well known locally owned fine restaurants of the past—Anna Maude's, Glen's Hickory Inn, Shipman's, Bishops, Doloris, Lady Classen, El Charito, and others? Unfortunately they no longer are with us.

However, one that still exists is Sleepy Hollow, still hidden away in a wooded area at 1101 Northeast Fiftieth Street. The restaurant specializes in pan-fried chicken with all the trimmings as well as steak, fish, ribs, and other items.

Eula Erixon whose only job experience was in the governmental and legal field serving as an assistant to the attorney general of Oklahoma, and who had never worked in a restaurant in her life created Sleepy Hollow.

Cooking was a hobby with her, and she enjoyed having guests and feeding them her home-style chicken. As a result, Sleepy Hollow was born.

It became a favorite place for state officials to bring out-of-state dignitaries and was equally popular among the business community.

Its present owner, Bruce Kliewer, worked as a clerk and busboy for Val Gene's Restaurant at Penn Square while attending Central State College. After several years with that restaurant in different positions, he became a consultant for restaurants facing problems. In 1996 he purchased Sleepy Hollow.

It remains a favorite spot for relaxed dining and has hosted such governmental leaders as Frank Keating, George Nigh, Henry Bellmon and others. Visiting celebrities have included Rock Hudson, Robert Stack, and Charlton Heston, to name just a few.

Not since early days after Capital removal to Oklahoma City has a hotel played as important a role in state government as the Ramada Inn and Conference Center, formerly Lincoln Plaza.

Its location at 4345 Lincoln Boulevard, barely two miles north of the State Capitol complex, makes it a natural spot for legislators, lobbyists, official receptions, and conventions.

It has hosted national and international celebrities, ranging from top governmental officials to well known entertainers, including Elvis Presley and Jane Fonda, to name just a few.

The project began in 1966 with an office complex. The conference center, attached through a passageway to the office complex, was completed four years later. The hotel to its south was opened in 1974.

In 1982 the State of Oklahoma purchased the complex for housing state government offices.

A year later it was sold to a private partnership and renovations were made. Renovations included expansion of the plaza, a new hotel lobby, restaurants and a club. Soon afterwards the hotel was one of only four in the county to win the four-diamond designation from the American Automobile Association.

In 1993 the complex affiliated with Choice Hotels. In late 2000 Ramada Inn became its new management company, Janus Hotels and Resorts.

Look for more gridiron shows, dinner theater, train shows, art exhibitions, conventions, or meetings between lawmakers and visitors to state government. All of these have been, and will continue to be an important role, which the Ramada Inn and Conference Center will be playing in the history of Oklahoma in the future.

# RAMADA INN AND CONFERENCE CENTER

✧

*A front view of the Ramada Inn, formerly Lincoln Plaza, north of the State Capitol.*

# SPONSORS

# PATHMAKERS OF OKLAHOMA COUNTY

Each year since 1990 the Oklahoma City/County Historical Society has recognized four living individuals and four from the past as Pathmakers of Oklahoma County, in recognition of lasting contributions they have made to the county, state, or nation. In addition, the Society recognizes one person or organization with a Distinguished Service Award for a singular contribution benefiting the county or state. Listed below are those who have been recognized with those awards.

## Pathmakers

| | | |
|---|---|---|
| Ray Ackerman | Edward L. Gaylord | Justice Marian Opala |
| Hannah Atkins | Vince Gill | Henry Overholser |
| W. P. "Bill" Atkinson | James Harlow | Russell Perry |
| C. R. Anthony | Victor Harlow | John Peters |
| Dr. James Baird | Robert A. Hefner, Sr. | Pat Potts |
| Ralph Ball | Herschel Hobbs | Wiley Post |
| Kate Bernard | William J. Holloway | I. M. Putnam |
| G. T. Blankenship | Fred Jones | Allie Reynolds |
| John Bozalis | Ed Joullian III | Cleeta John Rogers |
| Paul Braniff | John Keating | Oscar Rose |
| Tom Braniff | Donald S. Kennedy | Angelo Scott |
| Mamie Lee Browne | Robert S. Kerr | E. M. Sellers |
| B. C. Clark, Jr. | John Kilpatrick | Nan Sheets |
| Anton Classen | Garmon Kimmell | George Shirk |
| Charles Colcord | Eleanor Kirkpatrick | John Sinopoulo |
| Jack Conn | John Kirkpatrick | Peter Sinopoulo |
| William L. Couch | Patience Latting | Dr. C. Q. Smith |
| Vinita Cravens | Solomon Layton | Lee Allan Smith |
| Judge Fred Daugherty | R. W. "Whit" Lee | Jimmy Stewart |
| Dr. Harry Deupree | Dr. Bill Lillard | Paul Strasbaugh |
| Marion DeVore | Abe Lemons | Bill Swisher |
| Mrs. Selwyn Douglas | E. M. "Jim" Lookabaugh | Yvonne Chouteau Terekhov |
| Stanley Draper, Jr. | L. A. Macklanburg | Joseph Thoburn |
| Stanley Draper, Sr. | Dean A. McGee | William Tilghman |
| William E. Durrett | General Raymond S. McLain | Ken Townsend |
| Ralph Ellison | A. S. "Mike" Monroney | Bob Turner |
| Harvey P. Everest | Judge A. P. Murrah | Dr. Jerald Walker |
| Dr. G. E. Finley | Edwin P. Nall | Ruth Wynne |
| Dennis Flynn | G. A. Nichols | Raymond Young |
| Mrs. C. L. "Mex" Frates | George Nigh | |
| E. K. Gaylord | James H. Norick | |

## Distinguished Service Award

| | |
|---|---|
| Charles Able | Oklahoma City Police and Fire Department |
| Charles Coley | Luke Robison |
| Warren Edwards | Stockyards Main Street |
| Robert M. Johnson | Pendleton Woods |
| Leo Mayfield | |